# Kabbalah
# for
# the Layman

# KABBALAH

Volume III

**RESEARCH CENTER OF KABBALAH PRESS**
*JERUSALEM — NEW YORK*

*for the*

# LAYMAN

A GUIDE TO EXPANDED CONSCIOUSNESS

*by*

## DR. PHILIP S. BERG

FIRST EDITION
March 1988

ISBN 0-943688-69-8 (Hardcover)
0-943688-70-1 (Softcover)

*For further information, address:*
RESEARCH CENTRE OF KABBALAH
200 PARK AVENUE, SUITE 303E
NEW YORK, N.Y. 10017
—OR—
RESEARCH CENTRE OF KABBALAH
P.O.BOX 14168
THE OLD CITY, JERUSALEM
ISRAEL

PRINTED IN U.S.A.

The publication of this volume
has been made possible through
the generous support of
**NATAN** and **ESTHER**
**CHERA**
**SHLOMO, ABRAHAM, YOSEPH**
and
**YACCOV CHERA**
and
**CELIA FELDMAN**
and
Dedicated to the Memory
of
**CELIA BAT NIZHA CHERA**
and
**SHLOMO SALIM BEN ESTER CHERA**

*I want to thank my wife, Karen,*

*whose loving support made writing*

*less a labor and more a creative challenge.*

# Table of Contents

**Introduction**                                                        **13**

PART ONE
NEW AGE OF REALITY

**Chapter 1: Back to the Future**                                       **19**

*Time and the Infinite; Space an Time; Lunar Cycle
Fact and Fantasy; Sub-atomic Particles; Unification
Principles*

**Chapter 2: The New Age**                                              **25**

*Aquarian Age; Thoughts on Creation;
Consciousness and Revealment; Light and it Glory;
Bread of Shame; Body Changes; Endless Peace;
Never Resting Energy of Light; Eternal damnation
and the Messiah; Cosmic Code of the Bible*

**Chapter 3: Mind over Matter**                                         **35**

*Quantum Mechanics; Newtonian; Reality;
Cartesian Paradigm; Mind-over-matter; Creator;
Free choice; Fire-walking; Endless*

**Chapter 4: Altered States**                    **45**

*Drugs and Their Effects; Primal Cultures;
Negative Human Activity; Or En Sof; Faces of
Evil-receiving for Oneself Alone-Evil Inclinations*

**Chapter 5: The Speed of Light**                **59**

*Einstein's Quantum; Speed of Light; Travel and
the Speed of Light; Great Discoveries; Radium;
Desire to Receive; Sharing Concept*

**Chapter 6: This Modern Age**                   **65**

*Fear of Flying; Finite Life; Star Wars;
Emanations of Light; Complacency; Lower Seven
Sfirot and the Body; Encircling Vessels;
Illusionary World; Sensual Asceticism; The
Righteous Ones; Transitory Contentment*

**Chapter 7: Giving and Receiving**              **71**

*Moneybags; Circle of the Endless; Rationality;
Happiness*

**PART TWO
THE CREATIVE PROCESS**

**Chapter 8: Spiritual Substance**               **79**

*Existence Eternally of Light; Circles Within
Circles; Tsimstum; No disappearance in Spiritual
Substance; Light of Mercy; Space and Dimension;
Ten Luminous Emanations*

**Chapter 9: Mirrors of Redemption** 87

*Two Forms of Resistance; Spiritual Darkness; The Birth of Desire; Vacuum; Curtain and Bread of Shame*

**Chapter 10: Keter, Hokhmah, Binah, Tiferet and Malkhut 93**

*Illustration of an Optical Illusion; Hokhmah Wisdom Who is Wise; What is a Brainstorm; Binah-Intelligence; The Awakening of the Vessel; Light of Creation; Inferiority; The Level of Kingdom; Transformation; Light of Wisdom; Tiferet-Beauty; Small face; Higher and Lower Level of Consciousness; Ascent and Descent; Malkhut-Kingdom; Space; Reflection and Action; The Middle Point; Depravation*

**Chapter 11: Keter Vs. Malkhut** 109

*The Four Phases; Second Exertion; Emanated*

**Chapter 12: The Outer Space Connection** 115

*Knowing and Metaphysical Connection; Outer Space; Realists; Ten not Nine*

**PART THREE
EXPANDING CONSCIOUSNESS**

**Chapter 13: The Line** 123

*Capacity of Light; The Lights of Life and Spirit; Light of Nefesh; The Line Connects the Circles; Circular Sefira; Earth's Gravity; Here and Now Or En Sof*

**Chapter 14: Restoring Light to The Seven of the Circles   135**

*After Tsimtsum; Positive Blessings; Light needs of Darkness; Illusion from the Lower Sefirot; Proximity of the Endless;*

**Chapter 15: Activating the Central Column                141**

*Operations of the Universe; Restriction as energy; Returning Light; Resistance; Reflective Light; Newtonian Physics; Binding by Striking; Logic and Common Sense; The Filament; Circuitry; Encircling Light; Straight Light; Revelation; Process in Sharing; Examples of Life Situations; Free will or Determinism; Rock has no Free Will*

**Chapter 16: The Good Fight                              151**

*Justification of Violence; Our Beloved Ancestors; Karmic Correction; The Global Village; Peaceful coexistence; Reality and the Fourth Phase of Existence; Soul and Life Eternal*

**Chapter 17: Tikune, Zaddik, Coming Full Circle          159**

*New Channels of Experience; Blissfulness as Light; The Mother of Invention; Action initiates results; Growth; Seed and the Root; Endless Prior to Tsimstum; Zaddik Resistance of Bodily delights; Klippot; First Sefirot; Cosmic Awareness to Restriction; Coming Full Circle; Spiritual Circuitry; Negative and Positive polarities; Illusion of Lack; A world of Difference; Purer Levels; Existence and Free Will; Aspiration of the Light*

## PART FOUR
## ART OF LIVING

**Chapter 18: The One Percent Solution** 175

*99.4% Pure; Why are we blind to Reality; Evil as Illusion; Messianic Age; The Shortest Distance Between Two Points; Success and Failure; Creation of Affinity; Permanent and Temporary Remnant; Finite Nature of Things; Knowledge and Energy; Spiritual Correction; Removal of Bread of Shame; All Vibration is Music; Sound as a Channel; Creative Disengagement; On Death and Dying; Did Moses Die? Physical Death; Two Points of View; Encircling Vessels*

**Chapter 19: The Candlemaker** 191

*Wax or diamonds*

**Chapter 20: Crime and Punishment** 199

*Is there remuneration in crime? Fulfillment by rejection; A Fable of Two Brothers; Difficult roads; Beating of a righteous man*

**Chapter 21: Victim of circumstances** 217

*Hand to Mouth survival; A Man's Worth; What is Love? What is Lack? Amnesia; Limitation; The Vacuum; On Becoming Unreasonable*

**Post-Script: I'll take the High Road...**     **229**

*Two forces; The High Road and the Low Road;
The Path to the sefirotic triumvirate;*

**Kabbalistic Terminology**     **233**

**Index**     **241**

## ACKNOWLEDGMENT

I would like to express my gratitude to Robert L. Fisher for compiling and editing the manuscript.

*— Dr. Philip S. Berg
New York, November, 1987*

# Introduction

IN EARNEST DEFIANCE OF ONE OF THE GREAT CERTAINTIES of modern times — that nothing can travel faster then light — R. Isaac Luria put forward a new comprehension of our universal and the speed of light. Indeed, only within the illusionary physical reality of our universe are we confronted with corrupt theories concerning light.

True light, as the kabbalist pointed out was motionless and timeless. All physical forms of light were merely limited manifestations of the true nature of light. Connecting with light itself permitted an instant and practical intergalactic telegraphic system. This indicated travel of thought energy intelligences travelling at a pace faster than the speed of light.

No reasonable definition of the reality of light could he expected to permit faster than light messages or thoughts. Joshua, however, by instant galactic communication stopped the movement of the sun.

Probably the most bizarre and incredible story of cosmic miracles is the one that marked the career of the successor of Moses, Joshua Ben Nun. While pursuing the Amorites at Beth-Horon, he directed the Sun and the Moon to stand still, and they did it, we are told, for the course of a whole day so that an Israelite victory could be assured (Joshua, ch. 10:14).

Are we then to assume, on the basis of the Book of Joshua, that at some time during the middle of the second

millennium the Earth's rotation about the Sun was interrupted
by the command of a mortal man? Joshua, speaking to the
Lord, implored this startling cosmic disruption before the eyes
of Israel, and these celestial bodies, whose cosmic DNA of
energy dictates that they move along their precise,
predestined, orbital paths, obeyed as if this very interruption
was cosmically present in their computerized program from
the time of their creation, and indeed it was. Joshua's halting
of the Sun and the Moon was no different than Moses'
parting of the Red Sea.

The story certainly is beyond the belief of even the most
pious in today's world. We all have experienced the solar year,
consisting of 365 days, during which the Moon circles the
Earth and the Earth rotates around the sun. So, the Sun and
Moon should come to a complete standstill simply is an
incomprehensible cosmic event, unless we can face the
realization that celestial intelligences, otherwise known as
celestial internal cosmic energy forces, can be and we are
directed by man in his altered state of consciousness.

If this sort of revolutionary thinking is acceptable then
we can proceed to investigate and ultimately understand how
there can exist the possibility of motion and communication
faster than the speed of light. Most physicists consider the
philosophical implications of these theories incompatible with
their understanding of space and time.

Considering the distances of 93,000,000 miles between the
Earth and the Sun, the Joshua's command to the sun,
travelling at the speed of light would still take eight and one
half minutes.  Scripture indicate this command to have
immediately made contact with the Sun, a tantalizing, absurd
possibility that scripture maintains took place.

Consequently when R. Isaac Luria presented his doctrine of motionless, timeless Light, essentially he advanced the theory that Light was the all pervading constant element of the all-embracing unified whole. Therefore, connecting with and tuning into this integrated, intergalactic network system provided instant consciousness of the entire universe.

Most recently, physicists have been obsessed with trying to unify or find connections among the known fundamentals forces of nature. Rabbi Isaac Luria already promulgated the teachings of a grand unification theory. Kabbalah taught that the ten Sefirot or ten energy-intelligent forces expressed and made manifest the all-embracing unified force known as the Light. All subsequent physical manifestations were and are the direct result of a universe that started out with ten dimensions.

Unfortunately, physicists still fear esoteric or metaphysical teachings. In my opinion they certainly have much to fear from Kabbalah. The billion upon billions of dollars that are to be invested in new Genesis accelerator machines will produce nothing more than a fragmentary view of our universe. Today, some scientists even complain that theorists have ventured into a realm so remote from what can be verified that science is in danger of reverting to something like kabbalistic mysticism, unseen dimensions.

The Kabbalist has always known who we are, how we came and where we are going. His teachings have one decisive advantage over the teachings of science. Whereas in physics and other fields of science, the layperson has always been left behind in its revelation, Kabbalah with all of its existing truths shall become the domain of all Earth's inhabitants.

Unfortunately, the way the present scientific establishment is growing, it is becoming increasingly fossilized by its own particular world view, super-string included. One cannot continue to create formulas and inject the ever increasing aspect of uncertainly and a fragmented view at the same time. This begins to limit our growth and increase a specialization that threatens the sense of wholeness. The purpose of our being also has been severely fragmented by individual egos, which come to make the scientific empire an individual power base created by the owners of scientific knowledge they, themselves, have created.

When the majority of the people are placed beyond grasp of true knowledge, then we are truly awaiting the Messianic or Aquarian age in which knowledge shall be the domain of all, not a select few.

The Kabbalah, itself, has been a jealously guarded secret, but the time has come for it to reach the masses with its simplicity, because in the final analysis, knowledge which is simple is true knowledge.

As stated in Jeremiah, "And they shall teach no more every man his neighbor, and every man his brother, saying, know the Lord. Rather everyone shall know Me, from the smallest to the oldest" (Jeremiah, ch. 31:33).

# Part One

# New Age of Reality

# Back to the Future

THE READER IS BY NOW AWARE THAT THE PHILOSOPHY OF
Kabbalah stands firmly opposed to many scientific theories
and commonly held beliefs. One such example is the
kabbalist's insistence that light has no speed, another is the
kabbalist's belief that opposites do not attract, and yet another
is perhaps the even more startling assertion that space is an
illusion. It should come as no surprise, then, that the
kabbalist's understanding of time is also contrary to the
standard interpretation. Time, from the kabbalistic frame of
reference, is an aspect of the creative process, the Line, and
as such it, along with everything else connected to the lower

seven and this world of limitation, must be considered illusionary.

From the perspective of the Infinite aspect of existence, the upper First Three, the space-time continuum is an illusion. Time, as we know it, the separation of the space-time continuum into metronomic increments, may be a convenience and even a necessity in the lower seven, the world of illusion, but it has no merit or utility in terms of the Infinite upper three.

Concerning the illusionary nature of time, Kabbalah, in this rare instance, finds corroborating evidence in the most recent scientific findings. Physicists now tell us that time cannot be separated from space nor space from time, that gravity influences time, that clocks run slower at ground level than high in the atmosphere, that the speed of a clock is faster when flying in one direction around the earth than it is when flying in the other, that time stands still at the edge of a black hole, and also it hypothetically comes to a dead stop at the speed of light. These scientific findings, while certainly at odds with what is commonly referred to as logic and common sense, are well in keeping with the kabbalist's long standing assertion that the commonly held presumption of time adhering to some vast, unerring universal rhythm, is a complete fallacy. If time marches on it does so to ten trillion — or thereabouts — different drummers.

Space-time exists only in the lower seven, the dimension of the Line. Only in the Line do we find hearts beating, lunar cycles, bio-rhythms, seconds, minutes and hours, planets orbiting stars in regular-as-clockwork cycles, pulsars pulsing with uncanny accuracy, and electrons revolving around protons according to rigidly defined schedules. In fact, the entire visible universe and even much that is invisible operates in an obviously cyclical and measured manner. Thus, from our limited perspective here in the lower seven it is only natural that we view the world of fragmentation, the illusionary world of time, space, and motion, as the "be all and end all" of existence. So ensconced are we in the concept of time as a linear, never varying absolute that to even consider other possibilities requires a seemingly illogical state of mind.

It is not surprising, then, that when the kabbalist tries to tell us that time exists as an integral aspect of an unchanging infinitely-dimensional (or undimensional) plane, that the past, the present, and the future are all present in the same time-space at the same space-time, we are apt, from our limited perspective, to consider him or her to be a perfect candidate for a mental institution. The idea that the past, the present, and the future are all parts of some unchanging, space-time spectrum is a logical impossibility, the domain of science fiction not of science, of fantasy, not of fact. Yet Einstein himself admitted that if anything could travel faster than light it would also be possible to exceed the speed of life, as it were, and hop backward in time, the reasoning being that as time stands still at the speed of light it would presumably begin going backward after that speed was achieved. This could never happen in Einstein's view because nothing could ever exceed the speed of light. In recent years, however, many sub-atomic particles that do exceed the speed of light have entered the scientific lexicon, though in fairness it should be noted that the existence or non-existence of these sub-atomic particles or tendencies has not as yet been factually established.

The kabbalist is not overly concerned whether or not the

knowledge of Kabbalah will or will not ever be scientifically validated other than for the fact that were the teachings of Kabbalah to be scientifically proven more people would gravitate to and benefit from the mental, emotional, and spiritual rewards that are gained through the study and practice of Kabbalah. However, kabbalists are certainly not holding their breath awaiting scientific verification for the simple reason that they have ample personal proof that the teachings of Kabbalah are unquestionably valid.

Kabbalah teaches that the thread of our lives is woven inalterably into the entire fabric of Infinity and that we have the capability of tracing that line backward or forward, traversing time and space, leaping from one age, one lifetime, to the next at the speed of thought. For the kabbalist, past, present, and future are indistinguishable aspects of the grand Infinite continuum. The real world is unified. There is an aspect of unification within the atmosphere, within us, within everything that exists in this world. This Circular condition is indicated on the physical level by the planets which are approximately spherical, the atom, air bubbles, the concentric circles that form around a pebble in the water, as well as the human eye, head, and face. The paradox is that the real world must, as has been well established, remain concealed.

Energy-intelligences transcend space, time, and motion. Only our finite aspects are caught up in the quagmire of illusion. Our Circular aspect, the First Three, is connected with the great Circle of Infinity. The lower seven alone are susceptible to the friction and pitfalls of finite existence. Communication between energy-intelligences is instant, transcending both space and time. By bridging the gap between the three and the seven a circuit of unification is achieved by which the kabbalist becomes sensitive to the entire space-time spectrum.

Just as the seed contains the past, present and future of the tree so too do we embody the entire spectrum of humanity from our earliest primordial beginnings right up to the ultimate physical demise of humankind. The real world is unified. Through the attitude and practice of conscious resistance it becomes readily possible to achieve an altered state of consciousness through which the time-space continuum can be transcended completely, making telepathy, astral travel, and past-life "regression" not mere possibilities but readily available realities.

From our limited finite perspective time appears to be absolute. We are so used to gauging our perceptions according to the ticking of a clock and the seemingly rigid schedule of birth, life, and death, that we accept the tyranny of the world of resistance as a forgone conclusion. The kabbalist asks us to remember that the Endless is beyond the jurisdiction of that which is finite and that by connecting with the Endless aspect of ourselves we can open the gates of Infinity.

Kabbalah teaches us a way by which to remove ourselves from the spiritually impoverishing cycle of negativity, struggle, failure, and ultimate defeat — which is what people ensconced in the consciousness of limitation consider death to be — and leads us to a state of mind in which we are connected with the Infinite continuum where time, space, and motion are unified, where past, present and future are entwined, where everyone and everything is interconnected, where here is there and then is now.

Be alert, then, and ever wary of the illusion that poses as reality on this negative phase. It a is trap, perhaps capable of ensnaring a hapless animal, but not a thinking, feeling human being. It is a prison, but like any prison it is one from which some, if only a few, will always be able to escape. It is a wall, one hundred meters thick and a thousand meters high, but when one looks more closely one sees that its bricks are made of illusion. It is a house of mirrors that perhaps at times can best be navigated with the eyes closed and the heart open.

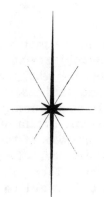

2

## The New Age

WHATEVER HAPPENED TO THE MUCH-TOUTED AGE OF Aquarius, with its promise of harmony and understanding, sympathy and love abounding? Where are the King Davids, the Joan of Arks, the Knights of the Round Table who held high the banners of peace, justice, and altruism? What ever became of the young rebels who created the great social upheaval of the 1960's — have they all, as the media would have us believe, traded in their rainbow of dreams for navy blue worsted, pinstripes and plastic?

True, on the surface it might seem as if the idealistic

fervor that fueled the fire of social upheaval in the past has been swallowed up by the ego-generated machinery that powers the so-called *Me Generation*. If we believe what the cultural icons tell us, this is an age of rocks and hard places, bottom lines, and money market funds. Hard economic realities rule this world, not some silly idealistic dream of world peace. The fadmongers, tell us that we are part of the *Now Generation*, and that this is the age of fast cars, fast food, and fast fun. Live for today, is their advice. Take what you can get, then take some more. The evangelical Bible-thumpers paint another picture, a bloody, gloomy portrait of death, pestilence, and divine retribution for any and all who do not toe the fundamentalist line.

Who are we to believe?

Kabbalah teaches that there is no disappearance in Spiritual Substance. Everything that is, ever was, or ever will be was present in the *En Sof* before the Thought of Creation — hence everything must also be here today, but unrevealed. Light, the eternal aspect of existence, is not subject to change without notice, it does not fade in and out according to the time of day or the change of seasons. The same is true of the great social upheavals that seem so ephemeral. In truth, important changes in the sociological fabric do not disappear, but remain indelibly etched in the collective consciousness. Like the Light that permeates every speck of material reality those changes in the social macrocosm are merely obscured, hidden behind the myriad disguises that mask the Infinite face of reality.

The New Age is here. We are beginning to witness, and, indeed, some of us are already participating in, a people's revolution of enlightenment. This spiritual insurrection will be made possible as a result of the efforts of individuals who are dedicated to bringing about a metaphysical understanding of the cosmos and man's relationship and place within it.

The prophet, Jeremiah, foresaw this abandonment of ignorance and its replacement by an overwhelming visceral comprehension of the very nature of existence.

"And they shall teach no more every man his neighbor, and every man his brother, saying, know the Lord: for they shall all know me, from the least of them unto the greatest of them." (Jeremiah, Ch.31:34).

Consciousness is a matter of revealment, a matter of simply stepping out of the darkness into the Light. The New Age was born with the Thought of Creation, and like all of creation it will be here until the cycle of correction has run its course. Man, perhaps, can change, by his thoughts and subsequent actions, some of the footnotes of history, perhaps, too, he can slow down or speed up the process of correction, but like any finite existence, the life of the human species must of necessity have a beginning, a middle, and an end. Hence, we, as a species, must one day shed our physical appearances and merge once again with the Endless.

King David has become synonymous with the advent of the Age of Aquarius and the Messiah. "In the days of the Messiah, there will no longer be the necessity for one to request of his neighbor, 'teach me wisdom,' as it is written, 'One day they will no longer teach every man his neighbor and every man his brother, saying know the Lord. For they shall all know Me, from the youngest to the oldest of them.'" states the *Zohar*.

As tenaciously as some people, who are ensconced in Desire to Receive for Oneself Alone, will cling to outmoded, violent, macho, ego-laden frameworks of consciousness, the fact is that the New Age cannot be avoided. It is etched in the cosmic blueprint, the map, the DNA of consciousness that was born with the Thought of Creation and will not disappear until the cycle of correction has come to an end. Like any living entity, the collective consciousness of man is destined to undergo a transformation before passing to the Great Beyond. The only difference between the Age of Darkness in which we are living and the Age of Light which is yet to come, is that in the Age of Enlightenment all entities and energy-intelligences will have total cognizance of their part in an eternal oneness.

By way of illustration, perhaps it might be useful to imagine a scenario in which alien spacecraft suddenly threaten to exterminate all life on earth. Immediately, all petty quarrels and differences would be forgotten and the sanctity and wholeness of the human race would rush to the surface of each individual's consciousness. Another apt comparison might be drawn between the New Age of humanity and the moments of supreme lucidity which often precede the physical passing of an individual.

The Light is here in all of its glory, the still, timeless, peaceful, infinite unity is present even in this world of greed and violent upheaval, but like all things that are real it must remain concealed to allow us the opportunity of removing Bread of Shame. Thus, kabbalists do not cower in fear of the coming Apocalypse, hoping and praying that they might be among the chosen few who will prosper in the New Age that is to follow. One need not, after all, look to the future for something that is already here today. Kabbalists gaze not into the future for the beginning of the Age of Enlightenment, they look within. The New Age is here today, as is the apocalypse, as is the pestilence, as is the final emendation.

All things physical have their roots in the metaphysical. Consciousness, not science, religion, or public opinion, is the harbinger of what is to come. There is no disappearance in Spiritual Substance. Nothing of value disappears. Shapes change, appearances, the body changes, but the energy intelligence never diminishes. The illusion changes constantly, but the truth beneath the illusion is constant and never-varying. Each stage of biological, social, and cultural evolution is impressed into the collective consciousness. In a like manner, each person's important mental and emotional lessons are remembered through the course of each lifetime, and his or her pivotal spiritual lessons are carried over from life to life. Nothing is lost. No great truths fall irretrievably between the cracks of existence, no great crimes go unpunished.

According to kabbalistic wisdom, the physical world is just a blip on the endless screen of reality, a temporary static disruption, a minor disturbance of the Endless peace, a pattern of interference which has existed only for the flash of an instant that we have lived as physical entities and will be here only until that time at the end of the process of correction when the universe fine-tunes itself out of existence.

What proof can the kabbalist offer to substantiate such seemingly outrageous claims in light of the fact that we seem no nearer to resolving our problems than were our primal ancestors when they first began to contemplate the Great Mystery? Indeed, if anything, the situation seems to have

gotten worse. Never before has the ecological balance of
nature been so seriously threatened, never have we hovered so
near to the brink of nuclear disaster. How can the kabbalist's
faith and optimism remain undisturbed with the specters of
war, genocide, terrorism, and nuclear proliferation looming
like dark clouds on the horizon of human consciousness?

Kabbalah teaches that we must ever be wary of
appearances — for things in this physical world are never
what they seem. Now, as always, the physical universe gives
every impression of being in a state of perpetual darkness and
chaos. The Light is here, but so obscured by the negative
trappings of finite existence that a sensitive eye and a
compassionate soul are required to perceive It. The kabbalist
is constantly scanning the human horizon for signs of the
Light's Endless luminosity. He sees It in the trend toward
miniaturization. Where previously a cable carried four
hundred conversations, a fiber optic strand can transfer four
hundred thousand. He sees It in the computer that once
required a large room but is now housed in a package that
can be comfortably lifted with one hand. He sees It, also, in
the quantum physicist's rediscovery of the so-called
"featureless ground state," which closely corresponds with the
ancient kabbalistic contention that the true nature of reality is
never-changing and perfectly still.

The struggle of science to achieve more with less is seen
by the kabbalist as a reflection of man's striving to shed his
garments of darkness and step once again into the light. Thus,
these developments, when seen from a kabbalistic perspective,
reveal an inborn tendency in man to strip from himself the
stifling raiments of physicality and to embrace the Infinite —
which, after all, we are all destined to do when the cycle of
correction has come full circle and we are liberated from the

harsh illusion that disguises itself as physical reality.

The Light never rests. It is forever compelling us toward the culmination of the cosmic process, the final emendation, the re-revealment of the true Reality, the *Or En Sof*. It incessantly urges us toward that heightened state of consciousness which will allow us to remove *klippot* and end for all time the need for Bread of Shame. The greater the Light's revealment, the greater the pressure on us to reveal It. What the kabbalist sees today is an increase in the pressure, a hastening of the corrective process that augurs the beginning of the end of a long, arduous process of spiritual adjustment and rectification, and the dawning, for many individuals, of a New Age.

Kabbalah, as the reader is by now aware, describes the physical as illusionary, and only that which is eternal and never-changing as real. Even today, the astute observer can detect trends within Western culture that seem to indicate a swing away from the corporeal illusion. Einstein's theories of general and special relativity caused a re-evaluation and ultimately the abandonment of rigid classical constructs involving energy and matter, time and space. Explorations into the subatomic world are revealing the dynamic interplay within the unbroken cosmic oneness.

From the kabbalistic perspective, the fundamental importance of these new scientific findings is that they provide a conceptual framework, a jumping off point, if you will, for realizing altered states of consciousness through which all separate manifestations can be experienced as components of a vast, intimate, and integrated continuum. For its part, Kabbalah furnishes the mental and emotional apparatus by which an elevated awareness of the interconnectedness of past, present and future, space, time and motion, can be achieved.

"Praiseworthy are those who will be in that age," states the *Zohar*, "and woe unto those people."

A common theme in apocalyptic literature is that of the New Age belonging to those who prepare for it. Some of the doomsayers predict that only those who have purified themselves will flourish in the New Age; the rest will, at best, suffer the throes of eternal damnation. When examined from a kabbalistic perspective this same scenario is seen as having not just one but several layers of meaning.

The kabbalist guards always against literal interpretations of ancient esoteric texts, and is especially watchful when interpreting biblical writings. This is not to suggest that a literal interpretation of the Bible does not make good reading, it does. And, indeed, it cannot be denied that the Bible provides a most valuable historical record. Rather, the reason the kabbalist probes beneath the surface of biblical interpretation is the result of an unshakable conviction that the real meaning of the Bible is not to be found in the "outer garments," the stories themselves. The meaning of the Bible, like the Light, must remain concealed.

The Bible, according to kabbalistic wisdom, is a cosmic code which must be deciphered. Every word, line, and passage harbors a sublime hidden meaning. Thus, to lift from the Bible certain passages concerning the Apocalypse and interpret them literally is, in the kabbalist's view, to engage in an exercise in futility.

Those who purify themselves have always reaped the

rewards of a New Age, a new life, a new level of consciousness; just as those who lurk in the shadows of negativity have always had to suffer. From the kabbalistic perspective, the Age of Enlightenment is not some distant, pie-in-the-sky vision of a new and better tomorrow. The New Age is here, today. It begins the moment each individual chooses light over darkness, good over bad, life over death.

As for the hellfire and pestilence predicted by the evangelical soul savers, yes that too is with us. Those who choose to live in darkness have always suffered a damnation, which, to the kabbalist's way of thinking, is every bit as insidious as any imagined by the fundamentalist Bible-whackers. The apocalypse happens when one has reached rock bottom, when one's life is in shambles, when some wrong has been committed that must be set right. The metaphysical equivalent of hellfire and brimstone consumes the mind, the thoughts, the consciences of those who have chosen to walk on a path of darkness. The world is strewn with the victims of self hatred, those who have perished as a result of the atrophy of their consciousness, those who are the grim reapers of the hatred they themselves have sown. The New Age does indeed belong to those who prepare for it, but not in the sense that the evangelists might have us believe. Those who do not work to purify themselves must certainly suffer the spasms of self-inflicted damnation. Those who cling to antiquated hard-line material views and values, the war mongers, the brass tack materialists who mistake themselves for realists, the power merchants, the ego-driven prime "movers and shakers" of the physical environment, will not, without major adjustments in their spiritual *modus operandi*, reap the rewards of higher consciousness. That, it seems to the kabbalist, is punishment enough.

Such is the age-old order of things, as it was, as it is, as it should be.

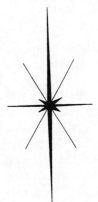

3

## *Mind over Matter*

A DARK CLOUD LOOMS UPON THE HORIZON OF CLASSICAL scientific thought and theory. Its name is Quantum Mechanics. New findings in the field of quantum mechanics challenge the scientific method and threaten to evaporate a mirage that has for centuries been generally accepted as reality. Physicists now tell us that in addition to the Cartesian paradigm, the foundation for modern science, which acknowledges as real only that which is subject to scientific verification, we must now consider a subatomic level of existence in which the scientific method is not effective, a world in which the consciousness of the experimenter cannot be separated from his experiment, a world which some say is actually shaped and possibly even initiated by the power of thought.

Newtonian and Einsteinian physicists must now, in light of quantum discoveries, confront the proposition that there is no such thing as true objectivity in any but a limited frame of reference. This, almost needless to say, strikes deep into the heart of the Cartesian paradigm, not to mention the ego of conservative physicists, everywhere. Objectivity is possible only when one can remain a safe distance from that which is being objectified. However, when dealing with the subatomic spectrum, the experiment and the experimenter operate as a single entity (process). One cannot be disengaged from the other. The experiment becomes an extension of the experimenter, and the results of the experiment are strangely dependent upon the experimenter's thoughts. Hence, we find a situation in which the standard *modus operandi* of science is invalid.

The kabbalist has long known that thought shapes what we perceive as "reality" every bit as much as that "reality" shapes thought. We are what we think. More than simply a means of perceiving reality, thought has the ability to create the reality we perceive. We are more than observers of reality, more even than participators in our earthly conception of what is "real." Thought, according to kabbalistic wisdom, not only determines the nature of the earthly reality we choose to create, but also molds the way in which we choose to interact with it. That self-created, tacitly agreed-upon reality is the field upon which we play out our cycle of correction. However, again according to the Kabbalah, there is, in addition to this tumultuous physical "reality," another timeless, spaceless Reality which operates according to an infinite set of criteria, beyond the machinations of the physical world.

This is the Reality to which the kabbalist aspires.

So well has quantum theory stood the critical test of time that all manner of accolades have been showered upon it, one of which has gone so far as to describe it as being the most perfect theory yet devised by man. The trouble is, quantum theory defies what for the past three-plus centuries has been the dominant mode of Western consciousness, the Cartesian paradigm. Named after its progenitor, the French philosopher and scientist, Rene Descartes (1596-1650), the Cartesian paradigm accepts as members into the exclusive club called "reality" only that which is subject to verification by the scientific method — which quantum reality is not.

This turn of events, of course, leaves the classical Newtonian and Einsteinian physicist, whose work is rooted in the Cartesian paradigm, in a very awkward situation. Either he must attempt to ignore the quantum theory and assume that the subatomic spectrum, and the rules that govern it (quantum mechanics), are not real — which, in view of the mountain of evidence in favor of quantum findings, is a practical impossibility or, he is forced to admit that the framework upon which his work is based, is not, as has been long believed, infallible. Small wonder, then, that many traditional physicists see it as being in their best interests to disregard, harangue, reject, repudiate, and discredit quantum mechanics in hopes that it will shrivel up like a dead flower and blow away — a fate for which — fortunately or unfortunately depending on your point of view — quantum physics is showing not the faintest sign or aptitude.

Unable to explain the efficacy of quantum mechanics, unable even to explain it away, the traditional scientist is faced with the unsettling prospect that there must be two realities, one that operates "above" in the atomic level, which can be explained according to Cartesian criteria, and another that operates "below" in the subatomic realm and is ruled by a separate set of subatomic dictates. Slowly, the scientist is being obliged to accept the fact that the laws of science do not apply to the metaphysical realm, and that, perhaps more importantly, he is being forced to abandon his cherished conceit of an objective reality, so arduously perpetuated — for the Cartesian reality is no more real, no more convincing than the Quantum reality. Each is valid in its own respective framework, each is real in its own right.

The mainstream scientist stands as one tottering at the edge of a black hole. If he falls back into the Cartesian reality, comfort and safety, he will never know what miracles might await him on the other side, but if he takes the plunge into the unknown quantum reality he might be forced to forever abandon logic and rationality and all he holds dear. There he hovers, on a tightrope between two worlds, two realities, one rational the other non-rational, one in which the scientific method is valid, the other which seems to be governed by thought. No longer can he cling to the misconception that he is a cool, impartial observer of nature. Quantum theory tells us that inside and outside, nature and man are one and the same. No longer can he maintain an aloof, holier-than-thou attitude toward the world. To do so would mean having to adopt the same attitude toward himself. And who can be impartial about oneself? Now, in light of quantum discoveries, the classical physicist must leave his ivory tower, re-evaluate the very framework upon which his thinking is based, adjust to a new set of variables, sort through and piece together all of the new data, and finally try to mold it into a viable and livable paradigm.

The kabbalist has no such problem to contend with. Kabbalists welcome quantum developments and even celebrate them. Certainly, to the careful observer, the quantum phenomena appears o represent a trend toward a return to metaphysical values, and in many ways seems to foreshadow the weakening of the centuries-old death grip by which science has dominated its inventor, man. However, lest the reader be left with the mistaken impression that the kabbalist gazes in awe upon quantum physicist's discovery that thought molds, alters, and ultimately creates reality, it should be noted that this amazing "leading edge" discovery has been known to metaphysicians for as many as twenty centuries. Kabbalists have always engaged in what has popularly come to be called the power of mind over matter, but as mentioned earlier, kabbalists take the concept one step further than the quantum physicist, suggesting that more than mere participators in the metaphysical (quantum) scheme, man, utilizing the power of thought, can act as a determiner of both physical and metaphysical activity.

The kabbalistic conception of mind-over-matter, nonetheless, does not necessarily correspond or comply entirely with the popular connotation of that subject. Telekinesis, for example, the physical movement of objects through the power of thought alone, bending keys, stopping and starting broken watches, while certainly within realm of practical possibility, are not, to the kabbalist's way of thinking, worthy pursuits — the reason being that to engage in such activities is to play, so to speak, into the hands of the Cartesian paradigm. What, after all, is the purpose of bending a key or guessing symbols on a card, if not for self aggrandizement, entertainment, or to "prove" to some so-called "objective" observer, (who we now find is objective only within a limited, physical frame of reference), the power of the mind over matter? A far more productive use of thought-energy, it seems to the kabbalist, is to power the mechanism by which one becomes engaged with the Infinite reality, mentioned earlier, for by doing so one becomes impervious to the physical realm and its machinations.

When the kabbalist speaks of mind over matter, he or she is speaking of undergoing an alteration of consciousness, a transformation of the mind, from the rational, logical mode to the non-rational, "cosmic" mode which allows for the conscious transcendence of physical constraints. Thought can traverse great distances, can effect people and objects, and is indeed a tangible factor in the world around us. That traditional science can not yet recognize this is no fault of Kabbalah.

The concept of mind over matter is given expression and defended in the ancient esoteric text, the *Zohar*, in an important passage pertaining to astral influences. When Abraham, the first astrologer, gazed up at the stars he foresaw that he would not have children. The Creator told Abraham not to gaze any longer into the wisdom of the stars for he would have a son if he attached himself to the upper realm and not to the stars. Abraham, knowledgeable in the wisdom of astrology, recognized the impelling nature of the influence of the stars and planets on man. Using his knowledge, he deduced that he was destined not to have a son, but the Creator revealed a paradox regarding man's existence in this world. While man is influenced by external forces he also possesses an element of free choice. The stars impel but they do not compel.

It is possible to remove oneself from the impelling influence of the celestial bodies, and even to transcend, altogether, external constraints. All things physical and metaphysical including humanity, are possessed of two aspects, one finite the other Infinite. The kabbalist's task is to rise above normal, rational consciousness, which means removing him or herself from the confines of physicality, the finite lower seven, so as to connect with the infinite First Three.

Humanity's finite aspect, what might be described as the flesh and bones, is subject to Cartesian rules and regulations; the other, the infinite characteristic operates beyond limited physical jurisdiction. Only the former is subject to pain, discomfort, and death. The latter is part of the eternal. And whereas the former is rooted to the physical world, the latter, being part of the Infinite is free to merge at will with the Infinite. By consciously connecting with one's Infinite aspect — which is done by paying constant homage to the original act of creation which was restriction — it becomes practicable to transcend space, time, matter, along with which comes the potential for presentience, astral travel, and the instant alleviation of physical and mental pain and suffering.

Legions of people of all ages, from all walks of life, have reported out-of-body experiences. In fact, we have all engaged in astral projection, whether or not we remember our sojourns into the ethereal realms. Science, however, has no way of validating astral projection, or any of the other so-called mystical experiences, because the phenomenon of out-of-body travel, like quantum reality, cannot be grasped using the scientific method. Thus, the scientist, given the inherited rigidity of his consciousness, is forced to conclude that astral projection does not exist. Yet, for any of the many thousands of people who have experienced astral travel there is no question that astral reality is every bit as real as the one we experience in our everyday lives.

It is hoped that the reader will forgive a slight digression for the sake of clarifying why the scientific method is incapable of revealing astral, metaphysical, and quantum phenomena. The scientific method, despite its notable success in exposing certain aspects of the physical world, has, as quantum physics has demonstrated, proved incapable of evaluating that which is metaphysical. The simple reason for ⁺his can be found by examining an underlying principle of the Cartesian paradigm which is based in the mistaken belief that nature can be browbeaten, so to speak, into revealing her secrets through a method of willful harassment. The Newtonian scientist, in other words, jars, jolts, and otherwise interferes with that which he or she is experimenting upon and then measures the reaction. A similar technique is used by certain large-scale fruit farmers who utilize bulky shaking machines to compel the trees to relinquish their ripe fruits. Thus, we find that while practical in the world above the atomic level, the scientific method has proved ineffectual when dealing with the subatomic (quantum) world — the reason being that the very act of inciting the subatomic particles causes a fundamental transformation in the phenomenon which the scientist is attempting to measure. To determine the position of an electron, for instance, it would be necessary to illuminate the electron using light of the shortest known wavelength, namely a gamma ray, but the gamma ray, upon striking the electron, would catapult the electron out of its orbit, thereby making verification of the electron's position impossible.

Does this in any way prove that the subatomic world is nonexistent? Not for an instant. Such is the case with all metaphysical phenomena: Just because they perhaps cannot be verified using the scientific method does not mean that they do not exist. All that it does prove is that the method of measurement is faulty. By a similar token, as was hinted at earlier, scientific verification is of little importance to those who have been on the receiving end of a mystical experience. Astral and non-rational encounters require no scientific validation. Those who have astrally projected generally need no one to assure them that what they have seen or experienced is real. Those who have witnessed fire-walkers stepping calmly and with complete impunity through white hot coals need no empirical validation that the mind can exercise power over matter — as is certainly also the case with those who have undergone painless, bloodless surgery with no anesthetic other than a hypnotic trance.

Not everyone, of course, is given the opportunity of examining the feet of a fire-walker; or has undergone surgery while under the influence of hypnosis; or has total recall of each one of his or her sublimely liberating out-of-body experiences. Quite naturally, then, those people are apt to remain unconvinced as to the mind's ability to temporarily bypass cause-effect relationships and connect with higher levels of consciousness. For those who have no direct experience with — or simply no recollection of — the uncharted regions of consciousness, it is suggested that the tangible verification of the power of mind over matter may be simply acquired by directing one's full attention to the back of a stranger's neck. Almost invariably the subject will react instantly and often will turn to zero-in on the power plant from which the beam of thought originated.

Kabbalistic wisdom holds that we are comprised of two aspects, finite and Infinite. The finite aspect, synonymous with the body, is subject to the laws of Cartesian science, the Infinite aspect operates beyond the laws of science and, thus, may be compared in some respects with the subatomic realm. Physically, we are creatures of the earth, spiritually we are perpetually connected to the Endless. The finite part of us is subject to change, turmoil, pain and suffering, the other, higher aspect remains beyond the jurisdiction of physicality. Through the kabbalistic attitude of positive resistance a connection can be made by which the Infinite self is, so to speak, illuminated. By attaching with the infinite aspect, a transformation of consciousness takes place which allows one to rise temporarily above the time-space continuum, beyond pain and physical discomfort, above the machinations of the physical world.

## Altered States

THE DRUG PROBLEM SPANS THE ENTIRE SOCIO-ECONOMIC spectrum. Doctors, lawyers, athletes, corporate executives, workers, students, housewives — young and old, rich and poor, black and white — no one, it seems, is immune to this all pervading menace. Staggering numbers of people from all walks of life are addicted to prescription drugs, uppers, downers, valium, quaaludes, diet and sleeping pills. Millions smoke marijuana or take cocaine on a daily basis. Alcoholism continues to be an international disgrace. An estimated 365,000 people die each year in the United States alone of diseases related to cigarette smoking. At least as many are hooked on black market drugs, heroin, crack, angel dust, amphetamines, barbiturates — just name your poison — M.D.A., P.C.P., L.S.D., S.T.P. — street corner pushers dispense an A to Z of chemical corruption.

School children dying with needles in their arms, junkies stealing and killing to support hundred-dollar-a-day habits, mothers selling their babies — incidents such as these have become so commonplace that news of them hardly so much as raises an eyebrow.

As if the problems were not already bad enough, the black market is now being inundated by a new menace, the so-called "designer drugs." Concocted by amateur chemists from ingredients available at any local drugstore, these drugs are chemically comparable to illegal anesthetics, hypnotics, and psychedelics, but altered in such a way as to make them legal — so while the law regarding the sale of a drug such as heroin might carry a term of life imprisonment, the penalty for marketing a closely related designer drug with effects and side-effects that are equally as dangerous is tantamount to a light slap on the wrist, or worse, the law provides for no sentence at all. The judiciary and law enforcement officials are hard-pressed in their race to even identify these new, highly addictive and often lethal substances much less to pass laws against them.

Small wonder, then, that the hysteria accompanying the drug epidemic has reached epidemic proportions. Everyone from the president of the United States right down to the man on the street is jumping onto the "War on Drugs" bandwagon and woe to those who are unwilling to go along for the ride. Debates rage on Capitol Hill. Blustery, self-righteous congressmen and senators challenge each other to submit to urinalysis. TV editorials decry the shame of drug-related crime. Letters to the editor endorse the death penalty for drug dealers. Feminists vow to "Take Back the Night" from the users, thieves, and dealers. "Experts" voice conflicting opinions. Hardly a week goes by, it seems, when a newspaper headline does not proclaim the most recent "Largest Drug Bust in History". Rhetoric flows like water from a bursting dam. In the meantime more drugs are bought and sold than ever before, more money changes hands, more lives are wasted.

Since the early years in the twentieth century — and probably much earlier — politicians have been vowing to clamp down on drug traffic, vice, and other blights on the landscape of humanity. Police chiefs have been declaring new crack downs and get tough policies. Supreme court judges have been passing laws designed to curb drug traffic or otherwise legislate morality — perhaps the most notable example of which was the fiasco known as Prohibition — but the combined services of the government agencies, the police, the border patrol, and the military have been dismally ineffective in combatting the drug problem, as is evidenced by the fact that the use and the importation of illegal drugs has sky-rocketed with each passing year. Crusades against drugs come and go, but the drugs, it seems, go on forever.

Not surprisingly, then, the latest Congressional proposals which will vow billions of dollars to cut off drugs at their sources, to crack down on dealers, to administer drug tests to millions of government employees, and to equip the military and border patrol with high-tech radar systems and state-of-the-art helicopters, have been met with more than a grain of skepticism.

Perhaps we should pause to consider some of the possible implications attached to these new mandates. Where will the billions of dollars come from that will be needed to administer these grandiose schemes? Social programs? Tax increases? From the fund for environmental protection? Perhaps too we should ask ourselves how these programs might affect our personal, legal, and civil liberties. Will every employer be legally bound to administer drug tests? Will narcotics officers be empowered to set up roadblocks and to conduct house-to-house searches? Will all of our phones be tapped? Will we be interminably delayed at border crossings while every car is searched, every suitcase scrutinized, every pocket turned inside-out? Will we be forced to undergo spot checks or strip-searches every time we board an airplane to or from a foreign country? Will the Constitution have to be amended to make legal this new wave of paranoid oppression?

Of course no politician in his right mind would ever propose measures as stringent as these for the simple reason that no democratic population would abide by them. Yet, given the pervasive and pernicious nature of chemical dependency, and the tremendous profit incentive for those who deal drugs, measures at least as oppressive as these would be required to bring a problem of the present magnitude under control. Countries such as Turkey and Russia have relatively minor problems with illegal drugs compared to Western countries — yet, fortunately, few Westerners would willingly pay a price in personal liberty equal to that exacted in those countries even if it meant a completely drug-free environment. Given the prevailing conditions, then, it seems that the best we of the Western world can hope for are stop-gap solutions such as those represented by the latest government measures.

As is the case with so many of the predicaments that Western societies face today, no one, it seems, is even considering, much less addressing, the cause of the drug epidemic. Instead we look for symptomatic solutions. With our jails already filled to the bursting point we should be attempting to uncover the underlying causes of addiction, instead we spend vast sums to make more jails. With the criminal justice system already tremendously overburdened we should be trying to find cures for chemical dependency, instead we incarcerate more young users and small time dealers and relegate them to a life of crime.

Imagine a system where a drug addict is cured of his addiction by addicting him or her to another, stronger, more addictive drug. It happens every day a heroin addict is put onto a methadone maintenance program. Does it not seem counter-productive to attempt to cure heroin addiction by prescribing an even more addictive drug, methadone? Should we not try to find out what is causing these people to turn to heroin in the first place? Imagine a rehabilitation program that turns away those it specializes in treating. Drug dependence clinics regularly turn away addicts who are seeking treatment because of restrictive policies, red tape, or overcrowding. Imagine a society that allows people to be jailed for ingesting a relatively mild, physically non-addictive substance while allowing for the promotion and open sale of — and actually collecting taxes on — other far more addictive and debilitating substances. Such is the situation pertaining to marijuana versus alcohol and tobacco.

With hypocritical laws and Neanderthal policies such as these (no offence to the Neanderthal who were more intelligent than is commonly believed) is it any wonder that millions of young people have lost respect for the laws and the judges who make them? With elected officials seeking temporary, easy-to-swallow solutions is it any wonder that the people who elect them do the same? With modern doctors prescribing medications to ease symptoms even when they have not the slightest idea as to the nature of the sickness, is it any wonder that their patients attempt to solve their own psychic discomfort with similar symptomatic quick fixes?

As an exercise in futility, let us now examine some of the recent proposals which are under consideration concerning the battle in the seemingly endless War on Drugs.

1.   Throw billions of dollars at the problem and hope it will go away.
This, of course, will do nothing. The Law Enforcement Assistance Administration doled out $8 billion to combat local crime, yet in those years crime increased at a record pace. Federal spending against narcotics has doubled in the last five years, but more drugs flow into the country than ever.

2.   Undertake a massive propaganda campaign.
This will serve only to glorify drugs still further. Besides, such announcements have been on the air for years with little or no effect.

3.   Increase the number of street arrests.
This will create a greater problem in our already overburdened prison and judicial system.

4.   Stop drugs at their source.
This method, though currently in favor among certain law makers and politicians, is doomed for a variety of reasons, not the least of which being that the United States

has no diplomatic ties with many of the supply-side countries. Hence, many of the world's main drug sources will always remain beyond U.S. jurisdiction. Also, it will raise the price of illegal drugs, thus increasing drug-related crime as addicts will have to steal that much more to support their habits. Locally grown and produced "designer" drugs will fill the gap. Even in the highly unlikely event that these measures did manage to destroy every jungle drug factory and stop the importation of all illegal drugs there would still be legal alcohol to fall back on, prescription drugs, cough medicine, airplane glue, sniffing the last few whiffs at the bottom of aerosol containers, and inhaling gasoline fumes, which was, until recently, the drug of choice among certain natives indigenous to the Amazon region.

5. Follow the lead of countries such as England and Holland and legalize drugs and dispense them at low cost. This is by far the most sane, practical, and humane solution mentioned so far. This fact alone, given the prevailing belligerent fervor of our brave political crusaders, condemns it to obscurity. Still, though while it has little or no chance of ever being enacted, we will give it a cursory examination anyway, for it would certainly do a great deal towards stopping drug-related crime. Addicts would not have to steal to support their habits. The drug kingpins would go out of business overnight — for who would buy illegal drugs at expensive prices if they could have legal drugs at low cost? Fewer people would die of overdoses because the quality of the drugs would be carefully controlled. The inmate population would be cut in half and the burden on the judicial system would be instantly alleviated. However, drug legalization has one major drawback, it would not stop people from taking drugs and, unfortunately, would probably promote more addiction.

Simple logic should tell us that extravagant measures, no matter how well meaning they may be, will do nothing to curb the drug epidemic. Burning fields, spraying crops, assassinating Bolivian drug barons, cutting off aid to various impoverished Third world countries, increasing the border patrols, activating the military, throwing billions of tax dollars at the problem, propaganda, radar-equipped, nuclear-powered helicopters, vigilante patrols, more laws, stiffer sentences, larger jails, packs of drug-sniffing dogs — none of these proposals will have the slightest effect unless and until we can identify and address the underlying cause of the problem:

Why do people take so many drugs?

Simply stated, the transcendence of normal, rational thought consciousness is a basic human need. People will do practically anything to remove themselves from this negative realm of existence — and that is as it should be. The conscious, rational mind is a trap, a prison from which our higher consciousness knows it must escape. Our encircling vessels are crying out constantly to be delivered from this world of illusion and to be reunited with the real world of the Light, the *Or En Sof*. Transcendence of this dense world of restriction and negativity is as basic as eating, as natural as walking, as necessary as the elimination of bodily waste.

Since time began people have sought ways to transcend ordinary rational thought processes. Early man was aware of this need and instituted culturally condoned methods by which this transcendence and unification with the higher realms of consciousness could be accomplished. There was the Vision Quest of the Native Americans, the Dream Walk of the Eskimo, each of which consisted of long periods spent alone in the wilderness. Through socially accepted ritual ceremonies, prayers and meditations such as these, people young and old convened with the spirits of their "ancestors", achieved unity with Mother Earth, made peace with the forces of nature and deepened their understanding of themselves.

Primal cultures have always practiced methods of transcendence, songs, dances, and ceremonies by which they achieved altered states of consciousness. We of the modern world have no such methods or, rather, we do, but they have been forgotten, obliterated by rationality, covered over by the trappings of material life, oppressed to such an extent that few of us are even aware of their existence. What was once a rich social, cultural, and spiritual fabric has been eaten away by empty material concepts, false technological promises, and finally digested by the great, blind myth, Progress. Today, that once intimate relationship we had with nature has been replaced by crass illusions provided by a cornucopia of so-called "recreational" drugs.

Thus, drugs, at least those of the "recreational" variety, should be avoided, but not for moral, religious, health, or even legal reasons. The problem with drugs is not the motivation behind taking them, but merely the fact that they are totally ineffective. The most important grounds for abstaining from drugs, then, is that they are grossly inadequate for the purpose of transcendence — which, after all, is the underlying motivating factor for taking them in the first place.

From the kabbalistic standpoint that which is temporary is considered illusionary and only that which is permanent is considered real. Drugs provide only a crude delusion of transcendence. The "high" wears off leaving the user in a lower state of consciousness than he or she was in before. The physical world is illusionary — thought-consciousness is real. Fortunately, reality cannot possibly be negatively influenced by that which is illusion. Our Encircling vessels are connected with the higher realms, the super-conscious *Or En Sof*, which is Infinitely superior to the false reality inhabited by our normal waking consciousness. To connect with this higher world — which is our inalienable right (some might say our *duty*) to accomplish — normal, habitual thought processes must be transcended.

From earliest childhood we are subjected to tantalizing images of "beautiful people" smoking and enjoying the "pleasures" of alcohol. Is it any wonder that young people emulate what they see?

Although there are numerous methods of achieving altered states of consciousness, Western societies have replaced them all with intoxicants. It is unfortunate that more people are not aware of other, more effective, methods of transcendence, such as those provided by Kabbalah. If everyone were to study Kabbalah no laws against drugs would be necessary. The growers would stop growing drugs for there would be no one to buy their deadly harvest. Smugglers would stop smuggling. The Mafia dons would abandon the drug trade because it would no longer be profitable. Perhaps then the Bolivian peasants could return, without fear of retribution, to their traditional use of coca leaves which have been chewed for energy in a manner similar to the way people of Western societies drink coffee — a practice that has gone on for thousands of years with few deleterious effects.

Addicts are slaves of illusion, but for this they should not be condemned. In fact, perhaps the addict might exact some

small comfort from that fact that even after prolonged
exposure to television, media, advertizing, the stultifying
confines of our educational system — barely to mention the
illusionary "reality" provided by a constant diet of drugs — his
or her instincts are not so eroded as to at least aspire to some
kind of union with a higher consciousness. This is more than
can be said for some of the politicians, law makers, and
bureaucrats who are concocting some of the grandiose,
symptomatic schemes mentioned earlier. They too are slaves,
the legislators of morality, the servants of rationality, the
worshippers of the false security provided by Malkhut, totally
and irrevocably imprisoned by the illusion of a singular,
stiflingly narrow perspective of "Reality." At least the drug
taker's soul cries out to transcend this negative realm. Many
so-called "realists" have lost even that capacity.

Negative human activity does not extend beyond Malkhut.
Humanity, thankfully, cannot cause chaos in upper (inner)
realms. Thus, our thoughts, if tempered by positive
resistance, are virtually impervious to the petty machinations
of those who are possessed by Desire to Receive for Oneself
Alone.

Kabbalistically speaking, being in an altered state of
consciousness means having no need for the creative illusion
provided by the lower seven sefirot. It means connecting with
the *Or En Sof* for the purpose of "seeing what is born." By
transforming the Desire to Receive for Oneself Alone into
Desire for the Sake of Sharing one rises above the confines of
the lower seven and connects with the First Three. Through
conscious restriction one can conquer the negative aspect of
Desire and achieve an altered state of consciousness that is
above and beyond the negativity of this phase.

The illusion of negative space is here for a very real purpose, and that is to allow us the opportunity of bridging the gap between ourselves and the ultimate reality of the Light, the *Or En Sof*. Through conscious resistance and restriction one can transform the Desire to Receive for Oneself Alone into Desire for the Sake of Sharing.

What is needed, then, are not new laws or stricter policies, but sane, socially condoned and approved methods of transcendence. Music can be such a method, writing, study, sports, certain forms of meditation, dance — in fact almost any activity can help us to transcend this negative realm of existence, but only if it is accompanied by the correct state of mind, namely, an attitude of resistance such as that which is provided by Kabbalah.

**Faces of Evil**

Evil has a thousand faces, and yet it has only one. From the perspective of the lower seven, evil is like one of those miracle do-all plastic devices as advertized on late night TV. It can be sculpted, bent and twisted, adjusted, amended, edited and revised, converted, corrected, modified, reversed and flip-flopped. Mold it, shape it, wear it like a mask. Toss it like a salad. Shoot it from a gun. Con with it, cheat with it, hoodwink, rob and swindle. Tease it like a beehive hair-do. It lusts! It envies! Evil, what a versatile product. And, of course, it comes with a limited sixty second money-back guarantee.

Those are but a few of the false faces of evil. In reality evil has but one face, the thought-energy-intelligence of Desire to Receive for Oneself Alone. Everything that revolves around that deceptive, ever-changing face of Desire, everything that emanates from it, everyone who allows that negative aspect of Desire to prevail, falls under its influence.

Yet, evil has no life of its own. Like a puppet, it is a lifeless, bloodless entity onto which we paint the faces, and for which we pull the strings. We animate evil and give it substance through our negative thoughts and actions. As a result, we also have the prerogative of painting evil with an attractive face. Yes, despite its myriad dubious characteristics, even evil may be seen in a positive light. In fact, it may be said that evil is an earthly necessity, for it is only through restriction of Desire to Receive for Oneself Alone that the Light is revealed. Perhaps, then, we of Malkhut owe a small debt of gratitude to evil for allowing us the opportunity of absolving Bread of Shame.

Then again, perhaps we don't.

### Evil Inclinations

As strange as it may seem, it can be more difficult for a person who has few evil inclinations to connect with altered states of consciousness than it is for one who is constantly inundated by evil urges. The reason for this is simple. The person who gravitates toward evil has more opportunities for restriction. Whereas the one who has no propensity for evil is apt to be complacent and thus be offered seemingly few chances to resist the Desire to Receive for the Self Alone, the person who gravitates toward evil has many opportunities to restrict and thus earn the Light's blessing by removing Bread of Shame.

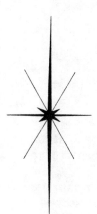

5

## The Speed of Light

IMAGINE THAT YOU ARE A TWENTY-THIRD CENTURY astronaut and that you have a device called, let us say, a "Lightning Speed-O-Meter" which gives you a readout of the speed of light as it relates to your vehicle. Logic dictates that if you are heading toward the sun the readout will be the speed of light *plus* the speed of your vehicle, whereas if you were heading away from the sun the readout will logically be the speed of light *minus* the speed of your vehicle.

"Wrong!" cries the scientist. "Not so!" adds the kabbalist.

In this rare instance the kabbalist and the scientist are in complete agreement — but for totally different reasons.

The scientist points to the Michaelson-Morley experiment of 1886 which "proved", to their satisfaction, as well as, presumably, to Einstein's and a few million others, that light travels at a speed of 186,000 miles per second regardless of the motion of the observer. This means that as an astronaut you might as well throw your handy-dandy "Lightning Speed-O-Meter" down the waste disposal chute and eject it into outer space because no matter at what speed your spaceship is traveling toward or away from the sun the readout will always be the same, 186,000 miles per second!

This fascinating "fact" of science defies logic and so-called common sense and for this reason alone the Kabbalist would dearly love to embrace it — for as the student is by now aware, one of the main reasons for studying Kabbalah is to break free from the stifling net of illusion that passes for reality on this fourth phase. Unfortunately, though, the Kabbalist cannot accept this concept for the simple reason that the kabbalist does not believe in the speed of light, period.

A number of kabbalistic concepts are at odds with current accepted scientific theories and the speed of light happens to be one of them. So far as the kabbalist is concerned there is no such thing. The essence of Light is everywhere, timeless, all pervading, perfectly still.

Which brings us to a question that almost asks itself:

If light doesn't move, then what is it that the scientists have been measuring all these years?

An excellent question, for which Kabbalah provides an equally satisfactory answer. While Kabbalah does not even entertain the possibility of the movement of light itself, it does make ample room for the probability that there is movement within the light on the part of the vessels, the Sefirot. The Kabbalistic perspective, in this respect, is more in keeping with the new branch of physics that deals with sub-atomic "particles" or "packets of energy" called "quanta" and hence has been given the name Quantum Mechanics. Quanta are more accurately described as "tendencies" rather than "packets, or "bits and pieces" because they are not really "things" at all, but rather more like Aristotle's concept of "potentia" which stands somewhere between the physical and the metaphysical, potential and reality. In any event, quantum mechanics advances several concepts which startled the scientific community when they were first introduced, two of which placed before us the possibility that the true nature of existence is beyond the scope of reason, and a second possibility, namely that certain particles travel faster than the speed of light.

Einstein himself believed that light is a rapid-fire stream of photons. In fact it was his paper concerning the quantum nature of light for which he was awarded the Nobel Prize. He drew the line, however, at the concepts expressed by quantum mechanics, that a complete understanding of reality was beyond the realm of rational thought, and that certain particles could travel faster than the speed of light. Thus he felt compelled to refute their findings, though he reluctantly agreed that they seemed to hold up, at least where the sub-atomic realm was concerned, with his now famous announcement that, "God does not play dice with the universe."

Subsequent generations of Einsteinian physicists have held firm to Einstein's beliefs and are also loathe to allow for either possibility because in the event that these quantum theories were to be proved correct it would punch great holes in the beautiful illusion which they have worked so diligently to construct. Their theories, you see, are based on the idea that light has a fixed speed of 186,000 miles per second.

Michaelson and Morley, ironically, were attempting to prove or disprove the existence of "ether winds" — ether being a hypothetical inert and totally motionless substance which, for many years was believed to permeate every square millimeter of the universe — when they stumbled upon their world-shaking discovery concerning the speed of light which laid the mathematical foundations for Einstein's theories of general and special Relativity, the first of which was to emerge some twenty years later in 1905 to set the scientific world on its ear. Michaelson and Morley's experiment did also temporarily "disprove" the theory of ether winds, and the idea of ether itself subsequently fell out of favor until the quantum field theory, which was spawned by Einstein's theories of Relativity, presented a new variation on the old ether theme, giving it the title, "featureless ground state" a hypothetical vacuum of such perfect symmetry that a velocity cannot be assigned to it experimentally.

In any event it is not our purpose here to present a treatise on the new physics versus the old, but merely to show the dissention among the ranks of science as it relates to different perspectives of reality. Quantum mechanics veers away from the Newtonian position that the universe is governed by laws that are susceptible to rational understanding, and places it in the framework of the study of consciousness — and for this the kabbalist is grateful. It sees man as a participator, rather than merely an observer of reality — another concept hailed by Kabbalah — for this too has been a major tenet of kabbalistic thinking for the past two millennia.

And as for the idea, which though rejected by the religious mind of that most benign and brilliant mathematical genius, Dr. Albert Einstein, of blessed memory, quantum mechanics presents us with the possibility that something travels faster than the speed of light — yet another concept wholeheartedly embraced by Kabbalah. Yes! Most definitely something travels faster than the speed of light: Thought, consciousness, both have that distinct capability. Kabbalistically speaking this is possible for the reason stated earlier that the Light is perfectly still. The Light is one. Every aspect of the universal Energy-Intelligence is in constant, instantaneous communication with itself, everywhere. Hence, by creating affinity with the Light, by establishing a circuit, a circular concept, the distance of a trillion miles can be traversed instantly, which if placed in terms of time, space, and motion would translate to the speed of light squared ad infinitum.

## Great Discoveries

When one thinks of discoverers, inventors, explorers, it is difficult to avoid the Hollywood stereotypes such as that of a serious, single-minded Madame Curie, working tirelessly alongside her husband Pierre, to "discover" radium, or Thomas Edison, the brilliant inventor whose seemingly superior mind produced over one thousand patents. In fact, more often than not, great ideas, thoughts and discoveries come about seemingly by "adducent" apparently "out of nowhere."

Columbus was looking for a passage to India when he "discovered" America — of course this is the wholly erroneous European slant on the story as Native Americans had been living in America for thousands of years. Then there is Newton whose theory of universal gravitation is said to have come to him when an apple fell on his head as he sat under an apple tree. And let us not forget the famous cry of "eureka!" shouted by Archimedes when, while bathing, he "discovered" the means by which to measure the volume of an irregular solid by the displacement of water and thus was able to ascertain the purity of a gold crown belonging to the tyrant of Syracuse.

The vast majority of discoveries were the result not of research and dogged determination but stumbled upon, apparently, without the slightest effort on the part of the discoverers. The reason for this, kabbalistically speaking, is that there is, as the old saying goes, "...nothing new under the sun." Therefore, it is impossible to discover or invent something from nothing — all we can do is reveal that which already exists on the metaphysical level.

Why, then, are some people chosen to make evident the great universal truths while others reveal nothing? Simply stated, those who become channels for the Light are those whose motivating energy-intelligence is Desire to Receive for the Sake of Sharing.

*This Modern Age*

THE KABBALIST SEEKS TO SEPARATE THE WRONG FROM the right, the fraudulent from the true — not an easy task in this era of symptoms and false fronts, after thoughts and second guesses. The voice of the kabbalist is lost, it seems, amid the clatter and the clutter of TV and media brainwashing. Facades, illusion, outward appearances are the trademarks of the electronic age. Social conscience has been replaced by image consciousness. No longer do we purchase a home — today we buy the neighborhood. No longer do we purchase a car — today we buy the hood ornament. No longer do we purchase clothing — today we buy the designer labels.

Enough is no longer enough. In this era of fast food, fads, and changing fashions we will not be satisfied until we "have it all."

One might perhaps imagine that kabbalists must get discouraged at times, facing as we do the constant barrage of greed, hypocrisy, deception, and illusion that passes for life in this modern age. Nothing could be further from the truth. One of the main purposes for studying Kabbalah is to remove ourselves from limited frames of reference and this epoch of hype and supercilious conceit offers more opportunities for karmic correction than perhaps any other. Which is precisely what the kabbalist loves about this illusion we call modern life — there is so much to reject!

**Fear of Flying**

Students sometimes voice concern about becoming too Infinite, too Circular, and perhaps losing themselves entirely in the study of Kabbalah.

Of course there is no possibility of removing ourselves from this illusionary phase of existence. Even an ascetic who lives in a cave must come down from his interplanetary voyages for an occasional meal. Finite life has always been and will always be plagued by interruptions. We can never withdraw from this world, the reason being that our self-imposed exile from the Creator makes us constantly subject to the influence of the Curtain. Hence we find that no matter how assiduously we apply ourselves to transcendence of this fourth phase the Curtain will always intercede on behalf of limitation, and therefore there is no danger in trying to rise, as much as is humanly possible, above this illusion which we call Malkhut and thus meld with the Light of Creation.

## Star Wars

It is a virtual impossibility for an uninitiated outside observer to comprehend the ancient kabbalistic texts. Little wonder then that when a skeptic scans the *Sefer Yetsirah*, *Ten Luminous Emanations*, or the *Zohar* he or she will almost undoubtedly come to the conclusion that the philosophy of Kabbalah is, at best, an anachronism, at worst merely mystical poetry of no value in this modern age. What, the skeptics wonder; can an antediluvian "spiritual" system like Kabbalah possibly have to offer to this great scientific era of quarks and quasars, laser beams, black holes and star wars?

Yet when these same skeptics begin to study Kabbalah, when they begin to realize that the Zohar speaks of star wars and explains black holes more succinctly than any physicist, that Kabbalah advanced valid explanations of gravity, the neutron, evolution, and relativity hundreds of years in advance of their "discovery" by science, that kabbalists have been engaging in interplanetary travel for thousands of years, and that the most futuristic scientific theories such as the possibility of going back to the future, alternate universes, string theory, and the "featureless ground state" are old hat as far as Kabbalah is concerned; how quickly and radically their skepticism changes to astonishment and admiration.

Now, instead of wondering how something so old could be valid, they wonder how can something so old be so new?

## Complacency

Kabbalah is not a go-with-the-flow philosophy. Kabbalists do not necessarily believe in turning the other cheek, sharing for the sake of sharing, charity for the sake of charity. For the kabbalist, complacency is a state of mind that must be guarded against, comfort a condition to be viewed with a certain disdain. This uncompromising outlook is sometimes mistaken for severe asceticism or simple mulish obstinacy until it is viewed from the correct perspective.

The kabbalist's seemingly implacable attitude is not the result of rebelliousness or rampant iconoclastic fervor, rather it might better be described as a temperament of positive resistance which results from the knowledge that no true rest, no peace of mind, can be secured until the soul's tikune, or corrective process, has been completed.

The natural inclination of humanity's finite aspect, the Body or lower seven, which is represented by all that is physical including, of course, the human body, is to succumb to gravity, which is the manifestation of Desire to Receive for Oneself Alone. Our Infinite aspect, however, the Head or First Three, which is synonymous with the soul, is not influenced by that negative, finite aspect of Desire (Gravity) and thus the natural inclination of humanity's Infinite aspect, the energy-intelligence known as the First Three, is to perform whatever tasks that may be required to fulfill the soul's Infinite cycle of correction.

The kabbalist, then, denies the body's natural inclination, which is to remain passive, as well as the craving of the rational mind, which is to remain complacent, for the simple reason that the restoration of Light to the Encircling Vessels cannot be accomplished by following the directives of that which is finite, including the body, but only by obeying the Infinite mandates of the soul.

Thus the person who seeks cosmic awareness finds him or herself in the paradoxical situation of having to deny the body's inclination which is to rest, in favor of achieving true spiritual respite, the Infinite stillness that can only be achieved by merging with the Endless — for true spiritual unity, the stillness of the Endless, can be attained solely by following the Line not of the *least* but of the *most resistance*.

Comfort, the basic energy-intelligence of which is Desire to Receive for Oneself Alone, serves no purpose other than to isolate us from ourselves and from others; complacency only sidetracks us from our true mission which is to reveal the Light. The kabbalist, then, gives thanks for the opportunity of discomfort, not to satisfy any masochistic tendencies, but rather to give the soul the opportunity for correction, which is, after all, the ultimate purpose of finite existence. Only by rejecting the desire of the lower seven for comfort and complacency can the purpose of existence, the revealment of the Light of the Infinite First Three, be effectuated.

Hence we find that it is not lack that the kabbalist seeks by denying that which he or she most desires, but the ultimate fulfillment that results from fusing with the Infinite. The kabbalist's attitude of positive resistance serves a very tangible purpose, for it is resistance alone that causes the disappearance of the illusionary world and the revealment of all that is real.

## Sensual Asceticism

The natural inclination of all things physical is to succumb to gravity, the energy-intelligence of which is Desire to Receive for the Self Alone. Our Infinite aspect, oppositely, the force that energizes the mind and gives light to the eyes, has no aspiration other than to share in the completion of its circle of fulfillment. Thus the kabbalist finds him or herself in the paradoxical circumstance of having to deny the body's tendency to surrender to the essentially "negative" force of gravity, and adhere instead to the more "positive" agenda of the eternal consciousness which is to return to the Light from which it originated.

As mentioned earlier, the zadikkim, the righteous ones of old, did not resist that which they most desired because of any masochistic need to punish themselves. Self depravation plays not the slightest part in the kabbalist's resistance and denial. It is simply that by reenacting the original act of creation, the Tsimtsum, one creates affinity with the Light and achieves the peace of mind which results from reunion with the *Or En Sof.*

Only transitory contentment can be achieved by succumbing to the body's every whim. Thus, the kabbalist chooses instead the path not of the least but of the most resistance, for only by paying homage to the original act of creation (Tsimtsum), which means rejecting the selfish desires which haunt our finite existence, can our infinite Light once again be revealed.

7

*Giving and Receiving*

GIVING, SAYS AN OLD ADAGE, MAKES LIFE WORTH LIVING. What could be nobler and more spiritually uplifting than helping the destitute, the hungry, the homeless? Surely one can achieve no greater reward in life than sharing with those less fortunate than oneself. True, helping those in need can be one of life's most gratifying experiences, as can receiving that which has been long sought and justly deserved, yet it is by no means difficult to cite numerous instances in which neither the giver nor the receiver derives any lasting sense of achievement.

Concerning the aspect of sharing, for instance, one is hard pressed to imagine a more thankless and wholly futile proposition than lavishing gifts upon someone who does not want, need, or deserve them. Examples abound of older men who are played for fools while attempting to buy with diamonds and furs the love of younger women, and of divorced parents endeavoring to alleviate their guilt by competing with expensive gifts for the love of their children. Such strategies, of course, inevitably lead only to heartbreak and alienation.

A gift means nothing if it is wrapped in a selfish ulterior motive. Contributing, even to the worthiest of causes, becomes a self-defeating gesture unless the giver is motivated by a certain sense of altruism. A business tycoon, for example, will find no satisfaction in donating even a sizable sum to a building fund if it is merely for the purpose of having a new wing of a hospital bear his name. Nor will a rich widow who gives one of her twenty-eight Rembrandt's to a museum retain any lasting reward if the gift is given for the purpose of receiving a tax deduction, or simply because a brass plaque etched with an inscription such as, "From the Collection of Mrs. Moneybags" will be placed longside the painting. A gift worth giving transmits something of the giver. If the giver does not experience some sense of loss or personal sacrifice, even an act of seeming beneficence is viewed, from the kabbalistic perspective, as a manifestation of greed.

Conversely, with regard to the aspect of receiving, no fulfillment, other than that of the most transitory nature, can be gained by receiving something that is neither wanted, needed, nor deserved. Consider the many sizable inheritances that have been squandered, and the fortunes that have been hastily acquired and impetuously lost through gambling. Easy money has wings — it departs as effortlessly as it arrives. Nor does hard work or even unfeigned sincerity necessarily guarantee protection from the pitfalls of conscience insofar as this topic of receiving is concerned. No matter how arduously one struggles to achieve some goal, he or she will gain no lasting gratification if the underlying motivation is purely Desire to Receive for Oneself Alone. Such is the circumstance concerning someone who steps on the necks of others, so to speak, as he or she claws up the ladder of success, or the thief who steals millions, or anyone who achieves wealth or high standing with no purpose other than greed, ego gratification, or material acquisition.

Thus we discover that the motive or intentions of both giver and receiver must somehow conform and coincide if mutual satisfaction is to be achieved. Giving is a two way street. A millionaire who donates a penny to charity will not benefit from the act of giving any more than will a poor man receive lasting value from a gift of something he does not want or need from someone he loathes. The gift, then, must please and benefit both the giver and the receiver if either is to derive fulfillment.

The truth of these examples become abundantly evident when we examine giving as it relates to the condition that existed in the En Sof previous to the Thought of Creation. There the state was such that the as-yet-undifferentiated Energy-Intelligences within the great Circle of the Endless began to feel a sense of disquiet at receiving the Creator's Infinite abundance while having no ability to give anything in return. It is pointless to give unless that which one is giving is well received. The Emanator felt obliged to restrict His outpouring of beneficence in order to satisfy His desire to share of Endless affluence while at the same time allowing the emanated the opportunity of absolving Bread of Shame. Henceforth, after the restriction, it became the prerogative of the emanated to accept the Light or not as was so desired, which is precisely why sharing, charity, and philanthropy, in and of themselves, do not necessarily benefit either the giver or the receiver unless those acts are accompanied by restriction, which pays homage to Tsimtsum, the first act of creation.

Mere sharing does not bring one to an altered state of consciousness. Nor does receiving necessarily impart any lasting benefit unless it is accompanied by an attitude of resistance. For the giver resistance takes the form of giving that which he or she really values and wants to retain, while the receiver, contrarily, creates a circular condition by wanting to receive but rejecting that which is offered.

This concept of giving away valued possessions, whether physical or metaphysical, and denying the same, is utterly alien to most Westerners and quite beyond the scope of what is normally considered by us to be "rational" comprehension. Thus it will never be understood, much less embraced, by those who are ensconced in Desire to Receive for Oneself Alone — which, of course, includes the vast majority of people. For those few, however, who seek a more meaningful existence than is offered by the materialistic precepts and dictates of Western societies it is suggested that this idea of resistance as it relates to giving and receiving be experimented with on a limited basis so as to experience its spiritual rewards.

Desire to Receive for Oneself Alone can and must be transformed into Desire to Receive for the Sake of Sharing if a circuit or circular concept is to be achieved — and, of course, as has often been reiterated, the only way to establish a circuit is through resistance, which in this instance translates to denying that which is most desired.

This is not to imply that the student of Kabbalah is hereby advised to give away all of his or her money and worldly possessions or necessarily to reject an Academy Award or a Nobel prize should one be offered. It is important to understand that the kabbalist's denial of that which is desired is not done with the intention of creating personal suffering or as an exercise in self-negation. Rather the kabbalist restricts that which he or she most wants precisely because he or she desires to receive all that life has to offer. This seeming contradiction is explained, kabbalistically speaking, by the knowledge that since Tsimtsum the only way to achieve fulfillment is through resistance. Kabbalah, when seen in this light, becomes not a negation of life but a celebration of it. Hence we find that even this concept of denying that which is desired must be tempered with restriction, for such is the nature of the paradox of resistance.

## Happiness

Given the circumstances under which most of us have chosen to play out our drama of correction, is it any wonder that many people are of a pessimistic frame of mind? To even suggest to many people, in this stress-filled age, that we have all the makings of our own unique fulfillment here, now, today, within ourselves — that we do not have to reach some financial or material goal or educational plateau to be complete; that our dream homes by the sea and all of the baubles of our illusionary fantasies, when once acquired, will do little or nothing in and of themselves to make us happy and truly satisfied; that all of our on-the-job training, experience, seniority, tenure, and university degrees play only walk-on roles in the quest for personal fulfillment, and in fact, in many instances, serve only to separate us still further from our real selves — brings cries of, Blasphemy! Heresy! Lunacy!

From the kabbalistic perspective, merely acquiring more and more money and material possessions in hope of achieving happiness is like washing a car that is not running well in hope of fixing the motor, like polishing a rotten apple in hope of making it fresh — and other futile gestures.

So what is the key to happiness and satisfaction in this world of resistance and restriction?

The answer is to change your mind.

# Part Two

# The Creative Process

8

*Spiritual Substance*

An IMPORTANT AND OFTEN REPEATED KABBALISTIC axiom concerns the fact that there is no disappearance of Spiritual Substance (Light) which means that it is impossible that the Straight Light that passes through the Circles disappears. And yet from the perspective of the fourth phase, the Light of the Endless becomes fainter and dimmer until by the time the Light reaches Malkhut it is almost totally eclipsed.

If the Light does not disappear, what happens to It?

The vast majority of this Endless Illumination is held in a

state of suspended animation, so to speak, by the phases of the Circles. By far the greatest portion of this suspended Light, which is in a state of potential, remains in Hokhmah, less in Binah, less still in Tiferet, until by the time It finally reaches this fourth phase, Malkhut, It is almost totally devoid of Illumination. The small amount of remaining Straight Light that breaks through to this fourth phase is repelled by the Curtain of this phase by the action known as Binding by Striking. The resulting reflected Illumination is called Returning Light, the effects and implications of which are explained in a subsequent chapter. The final act of revelation occurs when Returning Light fuses with the Light which is suspended in the Upper Worlds and all of the Light in all of the phases is at last revealed.

The Ari describes, in the following terms, the action by which the Straight Light descends to this phase: "...the Line, a straight illumination, acts as if it breaks the roofs of the Circles and passes through them (the Circles), and descends, drawn to the end which is the Middle Point." Of course we know that the Ari was not referring to space and dimension and nor do the Circles have roofs that might be physically broken.

The Middle Point is the fourth phase, Malkhut, which awakens Desire to Receive for Oneself Alone. In terms of the natural forces this negative aspect of Desire is likened to gravitation, as it relates to the human condition, it is equated with greed. Desire to Receive for Oneself Alone acts like a magnet to draw Straight Light through the Line that intersects the Circles.

Concerning the Light's descent through the phases of emanation, the Ari reminds us that, "there is no revelation of

Light in the Worlds (phases of emanation), whether above or below, without it being drawn from the Endless." Again, here the terms above and below have nothing whatever to do with physical comparisons but only to the degree of purity or impurity present in each phase. The Restriction referred to is the result of the Curtain of the fourth phase, Malkhut, which is also known as the World of Restriction.

The straight line vessels, the lower seven, intersect the Circles, creating an illusionary separation or gap in each of the Sefira of Circles. Although it does intersect each of the Circles, the Line also, at the same time, serves to unite all phases of the Circles, for were it not for Straight Light each of the Circles would remain separated in a similar way as each of the concentric circles that form around a pebble dropped in water stays connected to and yet sequestered from each of the adjacent waves.

Since the Tsimtsum reality has become revealed solely through the creative process called the straight line vessels, the lower seven of the Line are the only way by which we can make connections with the Circular world of reality. Insofar as we who presently dwell in the fourth phase are concerned, the Light of the Line (Light of the Spirit) precedes the Light of the Circles (Light of Life) the reason being that the Circles receive their illumination only via the Line. Therefore Straight Light, the Light of the Line, is considered more important than the Light of the Circles.

The analogy used by the Ari concerning how Light can descend from one phase to the next without any of the Endless Illumination being lost was that of the lighting of one candle with another, the first candle losing nothing at all. Furthermore, the Light descending might be compared to a lamp being covered with several layers of cloth. To the observer, it seems as if the Light becomes dimmer with each additional layer of cloth. In essence, however, the light of the lamp has not been altered in any way. In a like manner, the Light which enters this world, the World of Action, has already illuminated all of the levels in the Worlds above.

Thus, we find that the Light of the Endless does not disappear as it passes through the phases of emanation, it merely undergoes an illusion of concealment. Nothing is lost. The Straight Light must pass through each of the Circles, for as the Ari reminds us, "the Vessels of the Circles came out at once with the Restriction, but the Vessels of Straightness came out afterwards with the Line. Therefore this illumination which passes between them never really moves from its place, since as was stated, there is no disappearance of Spiritual Substance." The vessels of straightness merely give an appearance as the revealer of Light of the circles.

### No Disappearance in Spiritual Substance

That which is spiritual in nature is not subject to adjustment or modification. This is what the Ari was referring to when he declared that, "it is impossible that the revelation of renewed Light, which devolves through the various degrees, disappears from the first level when it comes to the second..."

This poses a problem in view of what we know about the lessening of Illumination between the levels of emanation. Hokhmah's Light of Wisdom, for example, is infinitely more powerful than Binah's Light of Mercy. The endless

Illumination is further reduced within each of the subsequent stages, until, by the tenth stage, Malkhut, virtually all of the original Illumination has disappeared.

As convincing as the above statement may or may not have sounded, kabbalistically speaking it is accurate only from the finite (illusionary) point of view. From the Infinite perspective the preceding statement was a complete illusion. From the Infinite viewpoint, the essence of the Light's endless presence is not changed, reduced, or in any way transformed by the process of emanation. Only from the dark side of the Curtain does the Light seem to have disappeared.

The vessel is capable of only one function and that is to reveal Light on the finite level. Each vessel's Desire to Receive determines the amount of Light that it is capable of revealing. Light is manifested in direct proportion to the Desire to Receive of the vessel. The three uppermost vessels, the phases of emanation, Keter, Hokhmah, and Binah (the First Three), contain only a minute fraction of the Desire to Receive found in the lower vessels, and thus the Light revealed by those upper first three vessels is practically nonexistent. Malkhut, however, possesses more Desire to Receive than all of the other vessels combined, and is thus capable of creating by far the greatest revealment of Light.

This is not to say the Light is increased by the vessel, only that more of Its infinite Illumination is revealed. Light can neither be increased by the vessel nor decreased. Each phase of emanation (each of which is a vessel by virtue of its Desire to Receive) represents both an increase in Desire to Receive and a decrease in Illumination — but only from the finite point of view. From the Infinite perspective the Light's endless presence does not decrease even slightly. The spiritual darkness perceived by those of us who have chosen at this time to dwell in the Kingdom, is an illusion which prevents our reasoning consciousness from experiencing the Light that fills us and everything around us.

Light is everywhere — and where could something that is everywhere possibly go that it would not already be? And so, while it may be a convenience to think in terms of the Light moving through the various levels of emanation, in truth, Light, does not move. Why should it? Light lacks nothing, it needs nothing, it wants for nothing, it has no need or desire to do anything but share Its endless beneficence.

This is what the Ari meant when he stated that there is no disappearance of Spiritual Substance. What is spiritual substance? Spiritual substance is all that is of the Light, which, of course, includes everything that is, was, or ever will be — except for one exception: The illusion of lack.

Lack and Desire to Receive are synonymous, inseparable. Like space and time, energy and matter, one cannot exist without the other. Yet, both are illusions. Only from our finite perspective do they seem all too real. The Light has but one aspiration which is to give of Its infinite abundance. It is only we, the vessels, who are motivated by the illusion of lack and saddled with its constant companion, Desire to Receive. In truth, meaning from the infinite perspective, we lack nothing. It is only from the finite perspective that we seem to lack the fulfillment which comes from separation from the Infinite Light.

Everything in this world, physical and metaphysical, was born from the Light. All substance is spiritual. Even matter, at its essence, is spiritual substance. Matter is only a temporary alignment of an atomic structure. The subatomic basis of matter is not of a material nature and is therefore not influenced by physical laws. Subatomic units, are called "quanta" meaning things, but are more accurately described as tendencies to become. And who can touch a tendency, taste it, see it?

Only a infinitesimal fraction of matter falls under the jurisdiction of gravity and the laws described by the physical sciences. This small quantity of matter, from the finite perspective, is deemed non-spiritual. Only that which is encompassed by Desire to Receive and must suffer through the constant illusion of lack is subject to transformation and seeming evaporation, the Light is constant and never changing. Spiritual Substance never disappears.

## Space and Dimension

So ensconced have we become in the world of illusion; so accustomed are we to thinking in terms of time, space and dimension, that it is impossible to rationally grasp a reality in which dimensions do not exist. Only by transcending rational consciousness can the higher realms of existence be perceived.

The study of *Ten Luminous Emanations* does not pertain to space, time, and dimension. It is only the inadequacy of language, coupled with the shortcomings of rational consciousness, that caused the Ari to describe the information that was channeled through him in words which seem to indicate that metaphysical activities evolve in terms of time, space and the linear proportions.

Thus, when the Ari taught us that the Line, a straight

illumination, acts as if it breaks the roofs of the Circles as it passes through them, and that It (the Light) "descends" and is "drawn to the end" which is the Middle Point, he was speaking of something that was well beyond the range of what those words normally imply.

Unquestionably, that which happens "above," meaning the metaphysical world, mirrors perfectly that which occurs "below," in the realm of the physical, but in Reality, meaning from the Infinite perspective, the metaphysical and the physical components cannot be separated, for indeed they are one and the same. The physical is to the metaphysical as one side of a coin is to the other, apart, yet at the same time together.

Hence the student of Kabbalah should be ever wary of words which seem to imply space, time, and motion, and to remind him or herself of the two perspectives, finite and Infinite, from which all kabbalistic concepts must be viewed. Only from the finite or so-called "rational" perspective, meaning as things are seen from the standpoint of this illusionary world, do words such as, "time," "space," "upper," "lower," "above," "below," "ascent," "descent," "physical" and "metaphysical," have purpose and function. From the Infinite perspective there are no distinctions, no differentiation, no time, space, no restriction of any kind. All that exists from the Infinite point of view is cause and effect, the cause being the Light, the desire of which is to share, and the effect being the vessel, the desire of which is to receive.

## *Mirrors of Redemption*

THE KABBALISTIC TERM FOR THE SUPREME PRESENCE IS *Or En Sof*, the Light of the Endless. When the kabbalist speaks of Light, with a capital *L*, he or she is alluding to that which is infinite and never changing, for such is the nature of the *Or En Sof*. A lower case *l* is used when referring to sunlight or artificial light which are finite.

The only *light* that we see, and the only *Or En Sof* that we perceive and experience is reflected. Both upper and lower case L/lights require resistance or restriction in order to be revealed. Like Light, itself, resistance takes two forms, involuntary and voluntary. Sunlight and artificial light are revealed through automatic, unintentional resistance, whereas conscious, voluntary reflection is required to reveal the Infinite *Or En Sof*.

Involuntary functions are rooted in the finite lower seven of the Line. Rocks, trees, the earth, and the animals are not required to exercise deliberate opposition to manifest the light of the sun. Obviously, a mirror is not obliged to consciously reflect the light that comes toward it. Our bodies, these finite vessels, are likewise visible without our having to constantly will their physical appearance, nor do we have to tell our hearts to pump, or remind our lungs to continue breathing. We are, however, required to impose conscious resistance in order to reveal *Or En Sof*.

Of all that exists on this earth, only the human species is obliged to exercise deliberate resistance to reveal Light. The reason that we are required to act intentionally to resist the Light is, as has been well established, for the purpose of allowing us the opportunity of removing Bread of Shame. The *Or En Sof* permeates all existence, but like sunlight it only becomes visible when reflected. To reflect the Light is to reveal Infinite Energy-Intelligence; to not reflect It means remaining in spiritual darkness. The paradox is that by rejecting the Light one receives It, but by accepting the Light that is constantly and freely offered, one is deprived of Its endless beneficence.

Concerning this enigma, a relevant physical analogy can be drawn between a black, absorbent surface, the motivating energy-intelligence of which is Desire to Receive for Oneself Alone, and a white, reflective surface, the energy-intelligence of which is Desire to Receive for the Sake of Sharing. The color black captures light, allowing as little light as possible to escape. So too does the greedy person, who is motivated by Desire to Receive for Oneself Alone, hold captive the Light that comes into his life, consuming as much as is humanly possible while giving little in return. The color white, contrarily, reflects light, thus sharing illumination with any and all that happens to be in its immediate proximity. Thus, it is said that the person whose motivating energy-intelligence is Desire to Receive for the Sake of Sharing emulates the white, reflective surface, accepting only what is necessary for sustenance and sharing all that remains, while the person who is controlled by Desire to Receive for Oneself Alone may be said to imitate the color black.

This phenomenon becomes particularly dramatic (in the physical world) at sunrise and again at twilight when the sun is near the horizon. At such times dark surfaces and all that surround them become invisible, while light-colored surfaces and everything in their proximity remain distinctly visible. Spiritually, a similar situation exists relative to the individual whose primary motivating influence is the desire to share. By resisting the Light, reflecting It, his or her inner motivation is recognized by all who bask in the nimbus of Light which is created by their resistance, while the opposite is true of the person whose motivating energy-intelligence is Desire to Receive for Oneself Alone, for he or she reflects no Light and thus becomes spiritually invisible in dark shadows of his or her own making.

Hence, the kabbalist acts always in the manner of a reflective surface, resisting, opposing that which he or she most desires, holding up a mirror of redemption so that the Light may be revealed.

**The Birth of Desire**

When the Creator withdrew He created a vacuum, a dark, negative void, that demanded to be filled. Of necessity, this vacuum manifested itself in every phase and facet of the physical aspect of existence. And since that time no Light is revealed in the created world (from the finite perspective) without a vessel, the motivating influence of which is Desire to Receive.

We are creatures of the Light. We were born from Light and to Light we must one day return. And therein lies the key to understanding Desire. All that materialized at the Tsimtsum, every speck of matter and cosmic dust, emerged with a need, a void that demands fulfillment. That void is the essence of all desire. And the need to fill the void that exists between ourselves and the Creator is the basis for all yearnings, psychological, physical, emotional, and spiritual.

We all have a vacuum in our lives, an emptiness that cries out to be filled. Is this any wonder? Having known unity with the Source it is only natural that we can have no rest until we are again united with the Light.

How is this accomplished?

Remember: The vacuum was an illusion created by the Emanator to give us the opportunity of absolving Bread of Shame. In Reality, nothing was changed by the Tsimtsum, except for the illusion, that which is seen from the dark side of the Curtain. From the Infinite perspective, the vacuum,

the space (all space), does not exist. We have no lack. There is
no void to fill. Only from the finite perspective does the
vacuum sometimes seem to exercise power over us. From the
Infinite perspective we are still, even now, filled with Endless
abundance.

The key, then, is to understand the ephemeral nature of
desire and to deny it access into our lives. The method by
which this is made possible begins and ends with voluntary
resistance. Seeing the illusion of lack for what it is, a
temporary apparition that disappears when confronted with
infinite reality, we must act always in the manner of a third
column, an intermediary between the darkness and the Light.

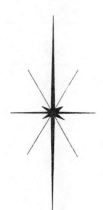

## *Keter, Hokhmah, Binah, Tiferet and Malkhut*

KETER MEANS CROWN. THE ROOT OF EACH LEVEL IS called Crown from the word "crowning," meaning "surrounding," which is why Keter is said to surround the entire "face" or "countenance" from above. Keter is the purest of all levels, and at the same time the most ambiguous — ambiguous in the sense that from our limited perspective it seems to change from Light to Vessel and back again according to the point of view from which it is perceived. Like an optical illusion Keter is one thing and then it is another and though mentally we can easily grasp the fact that it is two things at once we are incapable from our finite point of view of encompassing both "realities" at the same time.

When a king is wearing a crown we easily identify him as a ruler and thus impart to him the image of royalty, but without it, when he is walking among the common folk in common attire, we have no way of distinguishing him from any one of his subjects. Another analogy is often drawn likening Keter with the seed of a tree, in that it, too, can be seen as belonging conceptually in two places at the same time: the tree that was and the tree that is yet to come. Keter, because of this ambiguity, seems uncertain whether it is in its original domain or if it is part of the next generation, and we, from our limited perspective, have no way of making that determination.

A long-standing debate rages among kabbalists as to whether Keter should be considered Light or Vessel. If Keter is Vessel then it is the first vessel and can be aptly likened to the first seed that creates the second tree, whereas if we say that it is Light then it is a pure, total energy force, something divorced entirely from the tree. It seems to hover, caught, so to speak, between two worlds, that of cause and effect, energy and matter, potential and reality.

Still, though we cannot learn a single thing by gazing at

Keter's outward manifestation — indeed it has none — we can, however, determine certain characteristics concerning this enigmatic phase of existence by viewing the effects or manifestations that it creates, a methodology which is best summed up by the old adage, "As above so below." For instance, when we see a man or woman sitting on a throne in a castle holding a scepter and wearing a crown we are fairly safe in assuming that he or she is descended from royalty, or, by the same token, when a seed we have planted grows into a tree that bears apples we can rest secure in the knowledge that it was an apple seed.

Using this same conceptual construct we can say with some degree of certainty that Keter's primary Energy Intelligence is that of sharing — this must be so for it displays no Desire to Receive. Keter reveals what to the naked eye appears to be a complete lack of motivation. Forces of restriction, the Line, must act upon a seed before it can manifest its full potential. Only after we see activity taking place, the beginnings of a sprout or the breaking of the pod's outer covering can we ascertain that Desire to Receive has been activated — and then and only then can we call the seed a vessel in the truest sense of that word.

And so it seems that true nature of Keter's existence is destined to elude our finite understanding. Keter is the paradox personified, the enigma of life, and perhaps, from our limited perspective, its seeming duplicity will forever remain its single most salient identifying feature. Let us then be satisfied in calling Keter the connecting link, for any time we speak of Keter we are referring to the root of one phase and the crown of the next, to the transference of energies, to the linking up of time and space, energy and matter, cause and effect.

### Hokhmah - Wisdom

The first phase of the Light's emanation is called Hokhmah or Wisdom because, in the words of the Ari, "From it is drawn all forms of wisdom found in the world." Hokhmah is the purest of all of the phases of emanation. In the phase of Wisdom, the Light is unadulterated, unobstructed by even the slightest tinge of negativity. Its vessel is of such a transparent quality that it is almost non-existent, and of such an incorporeal and Infinite nature that its essence lies beyond even a master kabbalist's perceptions. Hokhmah, like Keter, defies finite understanding, and so again, as with Keter, we must interpret its cause according to what we can ascertain by studying its effects.

The ancient saying — "Who is wise? He who sees what is born." — speaks of the quality of Wisdom. Properly interpreted from the Lurianic perspective it means that a wise person is one who can look at a given situation and see all of its consequences, all of its phases, possible outcomes and manifestations, from the end to the beginning, the beginning to the end. As Rabbi Ashlag puts it, "... he sees all future consequences of the thing observed, to the very last one." And in reference to this he continues: "Every definition of complete wisdom is simply a form of "seeing what is born," from each and every detail of existence, right to the last result."

Unlike Keter, of which we can speak only indirectly, for the reasons previously stated, with Hokhmah, we at least have some "first hand" or direct experience. Sudden inspirations, flashes of intuition, these glimpses into our own unique fulfillment are the blessings of Hokhmah, but as stated in the chapter titled *Brainstorms*, they are only gifts for those who are deserving of them.

The Line is sometimes referred to as the creative process. Hokhmah, the second phase of the creative process, being one of the First Three, operates in a state of metaphysical potential, establishing contact on a metaphysical level with Hokhmah of the Circles (our inner encircling vessels) and causing in them a re-awakening. The Hokhmah of the Line arrives without our knowledge and stimulates the Light of Hokhmah within our Infinite Encircling Vessels.

All of the events, manifestations, and transferences of energy, of which we are now speaking occur beyond the dimension of space and time. When we speak of cause and effect in the metaphysical realm we are speaking of one energy following another, but not in space-time. We remind the reader that all of the Endless is in constant, instantaneous contact with Itself, everywhere. Only when the fourth phase, with its inherent Desire to Receive is aroused does time begin to take on a more finite, or linear quality. Before the fourth phase is awakened, everything exists within one, all-encompassing dimension, a dimension that might be best visualized by imagining an Infinite sheet of paper on which the entire macrocosm of history, past, present, and future, can be gazed upon at one time.

Notice now how "reality" suddenly and irrevocably changes when the perspective from high above the paper is shifted down, let us say, to the ground level of the paper. Here, the viewer sees only a minute fraction of the real picture. From this limited perspective the viewer has nothing to connect with other than the illusion (as it relates to the broader, higher, more complete perspective from above) and thus is apt to entertain nothing, no thought, idea, or physical manifestation, that does not occupy his immediate, limited visual scope and physical surroundings.

Does the reader now understand how a single "reality" changes entirely according to the perspective from which it is viewed?

Hence we say that Hokhmah follows Keter, but not within the aspect of time. In the Upper Worlds everything happens instantly. Events that seem to take time on this finite, linear, dimension, are, from the perspective of the worlds above, undifferentiated aspects of the grand continuum. As with all Kabbalistic truths, the person who wishes to grasp this concept must make a perceptual leap across the space, the chasm of illusion, that separates us from metaphysical reality.

**Binah - Intelligence**

The nature of the second phase, Binah, is the awakening in the vessel, the emanated being, of the Desire to Share. As Binah is a phase of "exertion" and therefore deemed "feminine" we might say that *she* is blessed with a gift from the Endless, a gift for which *she* has no desire. The simple reason for this is that the Energy-Intelligence of receival has not yet been activated — Desire to Receive being awakened only in the fourth phase. And because the Desire to Receive has not yet been aroused in Binah we find that while her vessel is filled with the Light of Wisdom, which is Light of the Endless, this Light which she would dearly love to share, this gift from the Endless which was inherited by her through the phase of Wisdom, can be shared with no one, for there has as yet been no awakening of the Energy-Intelligence of recipiency.

At this point in metaphysical evolution the options open to Binah are scant in the extreme. Here, she has been bestowed with a gift of unendurable majesty, but the Energy-Intelligence of receiving has not yet been awakened. In Binah there is no restriction, no Bread of Shame. She is, in this respect, a vessel that does not want to be one. Her sole desire is to share, to abandon herself unequivocally to the Light of Creation, but though she yearns for nothing more than to create such empathy with the Creator as to lose herself completely — she cannot merge with the Endless without forsaking her own existence.

Binah has no desire to receive — that grade or phase of will has not yet revealed itself. Desire to Receive arises only to fill a need, as will soon be made clear. At this stage of metaphysical evolution she has no desire to receive the Light and because of Bread of Shame she cannot keep the gift of Wisdom extended to her by the first phase. Only one option remains available to Binah, and that is to establish complete affinity with the light, but this can be accomplished only by cancelling out the thought activity of the vessel, which is tantamount to nullifying herself.

She has no choice. She must surrender. Thus, in the way that a young child abandons all pretense of individuality when lost in the arms of its mother, Binah seeks to satisfy her one desire which is to relinquish her own identity and merge with the Light of Creation. Having no one with whom to share her Wisdom, she disavows her very existence — as one might strip naked and plunge into deep water to cast one's fate to the sea.

This first phase of exertion or conscious activity on the part of the vessel is associated with Binah, and that consciousness itself is the root cause for the manifestation of a new transformation of Light. Binah's dramatic enactment represents a form of self-awareness that did not exist before.

It is through this very cognizance of her own being and giving that Binah transforms the Light of Wisdom into a light of a wholly different and "inferior" expression, the Light of Mercy.

Each exertion on the part of the vessel creates a denser atmosphere around the Light, and thus the Light found within each phase of the vessel is said to be "inferior" to the Light of the vessel before — though that adjective speaks not of the flawless Light of the Endless found within the vessels, but solely of the nature of the vessels themselves and more specifically of the degree of Light which each is capable of revealing.

The vessel, as it passes through the second phase, the first arousal, Binah, though conscious, is not thought of as acting consciously — at least to the extent that a vessel can truly be considered a vessel only after the fourth phase has awakened in it the Desire to Receive. The first three phases activate only the potential of the vessels, the fourth phase or grade of will, Kingdom, is the phase of the Light's revealment.

The yearning succumbed to by Binah, which leads her to act in supreme self-deprivation, is itself a "negative" Energy-Intelligence in that it serves only to separate her still further from the Light of Creation. Though Binah displays only Desire to Share — a seemingly benign and selfless characteristic — by simply emulating the Light, Binah is enhancing in herself an awareness that by virtue of her vessel she is different from and can never achieve parity with the Creator — so by merely experiencing herself Binah is changing her essence.

It is said that Binah's nature is to become and that her

consciousness is the thought of transformation. Binah, then, purely by virtue of her self denial, causes a transformation in the Light that results in an Energy-Intelligence that is changed to such a significant degree, so far removed, hence so "inferior" to the Light of Wisdom, that it merits a separate identity. The Ari, Rabbi Isaac Luria, named this transformation, Light of Mercy.

That this Light (Mercy) represents a significant lessening of the original Light of Wisdom, should in no way be misconstrued to mean that the Light of Mercy is comparable to the degree of Illumination manifested by the fourth phase, for the Light revealed in the phase of Kingdom is minuscule by comparison. No, Binah's is an awareness, an Energy Intelligence of such a high order that conscious entry into the phase of Binah is considered the ultimate state of metaphysical awareness that any emanated being can hope to achieve in this world — an altered state of almost total purity which can be attained only by an Energy-Intelligence that is completely devoid of any trace of Desire to Receive.

**Transformations**

The first extension of the Light of the Endless is called Hokhmah, the Light of Wisdom. The Light of Wisdom emanates in a flawless state directly from the Endless. It is the essence of the Light of Creation and the root of all of the Light's subsequent transformations. Hokhmah has only one aspiration, to spread the Light of the Endless, and hence it is deemed to be the pure driving force behind all existence.

No thought ever occurs the essence of which is not the Light of Wisdom. Hokhmah's Light (Wisdom) is the sudden flash of inspiration, the brainstorm, nirvana, satori, the highest state of meditation of which the most spiritual person is capable, the absolute joy of existence that sometimes comes over us for seemingly no reason at all. The Light of Wisdom contains both Desire to Share and Desire to Receive, though neither aspect is awakened until the second and fourth phases respectively when Binah arouses the Desire to Share and Malkhut awakens the Desire to Receive. Only when both phases of Desire have been animated can the Vessel truly be said to be complete.

The first phase, Hokhmah, the essence of primal perfection, represents, we might say, the Light "personified." He is driven by a divine inner dynamic of expansion. His one aspiration is to extend the Light to all phases of creation. Hence, he has no reason or desire to transform himself. In this respect he differs from the second phase, Binah, whose nature is to change her essence from Desire to Receive into Desire to Share — which she does with the intention of creating total affinity with the Light.

The Light of Mercy, the second phase of emanation, results from the influence placed upon the Light by the vessel, Binah. Thus, while Hokhmah was said to be an "extension" of the Light, Binah is named the first "exertion." In Binah the vessel attempts to achieve parity with the Creator. Binah is possessed of a cognizance of her own purpose that was not present in Hokhmah, and it is this very self awareness, as was expressed in an earlier chapter, that causes the Light to be diminished. As a consequence, the new Light (Mercy) borne from the exertion of Binah is of a lesser magnitude than that which emerged from Hokhmah.

Binah, merely by virtue of her own self consciousness,

the awareness of her own being, decreases the Light to such an extent that the Light that eventuates from her exertion is said to be a "transformation" of the original flawless Light of Hokhmah, even though the Light embraced by both vessels (Hokhmah and Binah) is the same Light (*Or En Sof*) of the same Infinite intensity as that which passed through Hokhmah. Thus, it is said that the Light of Mercy, is the same Infinite Light of the Endless "transformed" by the vessel for the sake of sharing.

**Tiferet - Beauty**

The third phase of the Light's emanation has many names. It is called, The World of Formation. It is called the second "extension" of the Light — the phase of Hokhmah (Wisdom) was also an extension — and is therefore defined as being "masculine." The second and forth phases, you will recall, Binah and Kingdom, are known as "exertions" and defined as being "feminine." Tiferet (Beauty), the third phase of emanation, is also called Microprosopan (small personification), or Small Face, because, like the moon reflects the sun, Tiferet is a reflection of a higher truth, the Light of the Endless.

In the Small Face — which is said to comprise two triads of emanations, the six sefirot, Hesed (Mercy), Gevura (Judgement), Tiferet (Beauty), Netzah (Victory), Hod (Glory) and Yesod (Foundation) — is an extension of the Light of Mercy that emanated from Binah (Intelligence) by which the Light of Wisdom is again made manifest. This third phase represents a spreading out and hence a dissipation of Binah's Light (Mercy) the thought or energy-intelligence of which was to transform the vessel back into the Light. Binah's exertion, you will recall, transformed the Light of Hokhmah

(Wisdom) into the Light of a separate description, the Light of Mercy.

As the student is by now aware, the Divine Light of the Creator was not concealed and therefore revealed in one action, but was transformed by a number of stages. The first phase, Hokhmah (Wisdom) had no consciousness of itself. Binah, awakened the Desire to Share, but concealed the Light of Wisdom through her desire to emulate It, and thus gave birth to a new transformation of the Light, the Light of Mercy. In Small Face the total negation of vessel as vessel is carried over from Binah whose desire was to surrender herself completely to the Light, but here in the third phase there is an added enclothement of the vessel. Just as we must dress our vessels, our bodies, in order to make our presence felt to others, the Small Face enclothes the Light still further so that Its Divine Presence, too, in a manner of speaking, can begin to spread Its message to the physical world.

The third stage of the Light's emanation, Tiferet (Beauty), the Small Face, may be seen, then, as the phase in which the Light of Mercy spreads out, hence becoming further concealed and dissipated from the point of view of Light, but closer to revealment from the perspective of the Vessel — like the calm before a storm, the third phase of emanation, represents a gathering of the forces of the universe in preparation for the tidal wave of revealment which is about to follow in the fourth and last phase, Kingdom.

**Small Face**

Desire to Receive is included within all levels and layers

of created existence. It is essential that every vessel possess a certain amount of Desire to Receive, for that which is lacking in some dynamic force of attraction could not possibly manifest or maintain any material shape or essence. Thus, even the First Three (Keter, Hokhmah, Binah) must also include a certain minuscule allotment of Desire to Receive, otherwise those exalted sefirot could not be called vessels in the truest kabbalistic sense of the word.

Both the higher and the lower levels of consciousness are comprised of the same fundamental elements, Light and Vessel, the only difference being in the aspect of revealment. From the Endless right down to this World of Action, nothing changes other than the increasing illusion of Desire to Receive for the Self Alone. The negative aspect of desire acts as a cloak by which the upper levels of our existence are obscured from what we might call spiritual view.

The Light of Wisdom is termed "Light of the Face," which according to the Ari reveals the hidden meaning of the verse, "A man's wisdom lights his face." Thus the first phase, the Crown (Keter) of the world of Emanation, which is illuminated by the Light of Wisdom, is given the name, "The Long Face," while the third phase, which is illuminated by the lesser Light of Mercy, which extends to the six sefirot, Hesed (Mercy), Gevurah (Judgment), Tifereth (Beauty), Netzah (Victory), Hod (Gloryy), and Yesod (Foundation), is named "The Small Face." The six sefirot of the third phase, Small Face (Ze'ir Anpin), are the realms of consciousness entered into with the aid of meditation.

Descending through the six sefirot of the Small Face the influence of Desire to Receive for the Self Alone becomes more and more pronounced. Each of the six is endowed with both the positive and the negative aspects of Desire to Receive. However, while a certain portion of Desire to Receive for the Self Alone must of necessity be embodied within the vessels of the Small Face, certainly this amount is infinitesimal compared to the negative aspect of desire that manifests in the fourth phase, Kingdom (Malkhut) where the Light of all subsequent phases is revealed.

## Malkhut - Kingdom

Malkhut reveals the purpose of creation. Here in the fourth phase the three previous phases are transformed from potential to actual, the dormant is awakened, the hidden is exposed, the passive is activated, the immaterial is materialized. Small Face dispersed the Light to such a extent that it caused a severe lack or deficiency in the vessel, an unquenchable thirst for the completion it once knew. That need for re-fulfillment caused the arousal of Desire to Receive in the phase of Malkhut.

Space — both in terms of the physical and emotional separation between people and the distance between objects and planetary bodies — is a product of the loss or deficiency experienced by the vessel because of the diffusion of the Light that occurred in the third phase, Small Face. This "distance" between the physical and the metaphysical was placed between the Emanator and that which He had emanated in order to preserve the illusion of separation that was a prerequisite of Creation.

While the revealment of sunlight takes place as a result of involuntary reflective action, the revelation of the *Or En Sof*, conversely, at least insofar as we of Malkhut are concerned, manifests as a result of voluntary resistance. The Earth's primal motivating energy-intelligence, the Desire to Receive for Itself Alone, acts involuntarily in conjunction with the nature's inborn restrictive mechanism (Curtain) to reveal sunlight. We, however, because of our wish for individuation, must reveal the Light through a conscious act of resistance or restriction so as to absolve Bread of Shame — for that was the purpose of creation.

Recall that no light materializes other than that which is reflected. As has been previously noted, sunlight is revealed only through an act of resistance (reflection). This fact becomes readily apparent by gazing into the night sky. Light does not manifest between the stars, planets, and heavenly bodies simply because there is nothing of a physical nature with which it can interact. Hence, having nothing to reflect from (other than nuclear particles which exhibit only minute Desire to Receive) light cannot be seen.

No light, no sound, no thought, nothing comes to Light in this World of Restriction without resistance, and the greater is the resistance the more magnanimous is the outpouring of energy. We of Malkhut must work to deactivate the Curtain and thus re-illuminate our Infinite Energy-Intelligence, which, from our necessarily limited perspective, lies dormant within our inner Encircling Vessels. Our separation from the Light, which was the purpose of Tsimstum, served to differentiate between the Creator and that which He had emanated, thus providing us with the opportunity of alleviating Bread of Shame.

**The Middle Point**

The middle point is Malkhut, the point from which

radiated all worlds of emanation. It is the place of first resistance, the point at which the world of creation begins. The middle point reveals the infinite circular vessels from which we all emerged and to which we will all one day return. The irony is that the only way we can unveil that infinite Circular reality is through the finite creative process known to Kabbalah as the Line.

The middle point reveals reality. It is our place of infinite, internal fullness and ultimate fulfillment. To connect with the middle point is to reveal the infinite circular vessels of our being. Unless one can reach the middle point of his or her own being, he or she is destined to remain always in spiritual darkness. For it is at the middle point that all Light is revealed.

If we feel sadness or depravation it means that we are ensconced in illusion. As mentioned previously, lack can take root only in the world of illusion, and only there can it survive. By attaching to the infinite middle point of our beings we cause the illusion of lack to lose its purpose in the world of illusion and, thus, having nothing of a negative nature on which to feed, it must of necessity disappear.

The importance of connecting with the middle point, humanity's internal place of the Light's revealment cannot be overemphasized. In fact, the middle point is generally accepted by kabbalists as being the fundamental difference between the spiritual and the non-spiritual person. For whereas the spiritual person understands that all blessings emanate from a single source, the non-spiritual person sees only random chance as the motivating influence of his or her life. Thus, while the spiritual person's life is anchored in the tranquil waters of Reality, the non-spiritual person is tossed about like a twig on a sea of illusion.

## Keter vs. Malkhut

WE ARE BY NOW AWARE THAT KETER, BEING CLOSELY aligned with the Infinite, is considered by Kabbalah to be greatly purer, higher, and thus superior to Malkhut. Yet, from the following imaginary discussion between two students of Kabbalah, we shall see that the two sefirot are perhaps more intimately related than previously imagined.

Kabbalist One: Keter is higher.

Kabbalist Two: No, I say it is Malkhut for without her there would be no revealment of the Light.

Kabbalist One:   Yes, but without Keter there would be no Light to reveal.

Kabbalist Two:   True, but both, after all, are vessels — so how can you say one is higher than the other?

Kabbalist One:   Which would you rather drink, sludge or distilled water?

Kabbalist Two:   All right, so admittedly Keter is, shall we say, of a purer consistency — but it is Malkhut's very density that allows her to reveal the Light — which was, you will remember, the purpose of creation.

Kabbalist One:   Maybe so, but Malkhut's main motivation is still Desire to Receive for Oneself Alone — which *you* will remember is the epitome of evil and negativity.

Kabbalist Two:   If that is so then why is it that only Malkhut and not Keter can have a dialogue with the Creator?

Kabbalist One:   Dialogue? Malkhut's only free will is restriction, saying *no* — is that what you call a dialogue?

Kabbalist Two:   It is better than what Keter can do.

Kabbalist One:   Keter does not have to speak. He communicates in other, better, more Infinite ways.

Kabbalist Two:   Ways that no mortal can understand.

Kabbalist One:   Only our finite aspect cannot perceive Keter, our Infinite aspect hears him loud and clear.

Kabbalist Two: Big deal. What good is that? What's the good of anything if it's concealed?

Kabbalist One: What good is the Creator, then, by that reasoning?

Kabbalist Two: That's not what I mean and you know it. I'm talking about here on Malkhut. Thoughts, words, deeds — anything you can name — what good is it if it's not revealed?

Kabbalist One: There, you said the magic word, *name* — anything you can *name*. If it's got a name it's part of the creative process, in other words, the illusion.

Kabbalist Two: That's the paradox. The illusion is the only way the Light is revealed. Besides, Keter also has a name, so it too must be part of the illusion.

Kabbalist One: True, but less a part by far than Malkhut. Even you must admit that.

Kabbalist Two: Maybe so, but without illusion we'd still be back in the En Sof trying to find a way to get rid of Bread of Shame.

Kabbalist One: Better that than being down here trying to get rid of the illusion.

Kabbalist Two: What's so bad about illusion? Books are illusion, records, plays, Alfa Romeos, bodies...

Kabbalist One: Hmmm. You've got a point there. Maybe illusion is not such a bad thing after all.

Let us leave our two students of Kabbalah to their discussion. Which one is right? There is only one possible resolution to this argument, the ultimate compromise: both.

### The Four Phases

The emergence of the four phases of emanation is often likened to the concentric circles that form around the point at which a stone is thrown into water. The first extension of the Light, Wisdom (Hokhmah), "the potential vessel," forms the outer circle which is said to "cause" the second phase, Intelligence (Binah), where potential is activated, which in turn causes Beauty (Tiferet), the first "state of arousal" (also called "Small Face," which is comprised of the Lights of Mercy, Judgement, Beauty, Endurance, Majesty, and Foundation) which in turn causes the fourth phase, Kingdom (Malkhut) where the Desire to receive is fully awakened and all four phases are finally revealed.

The first and third phases are said to be "extensions" of the Light and are represented as being "masculine" while the second and fourth phases are called "exertions" and are described as being "feminine." The two "extensions" of the Light, Wisdom, the first phase, and Beauty, the third, are each bestowed with Light extended from the Emanator — Wisdom with the Light of Wisdom, Beauty with the Light of Mercy — whereas the two "exertions" of will, Intelligence, the second phase, and Kingdom, (sometimes called "Queen"), the fourth, represent the striving capacity in the emanated beings. The first exertion, Intelligence awakens in the emanated being the Desire to Share, the second exertion, Kingdom awakens the Desire to Receive.

Of course, all ten sefirot are included in each extension and in each exertion of the Light.

Nothing exists in this observable world that has not gone through four phases. Thoughts, words, deeds, growth, movement, relationships, the manufacture or evolution of physical objects, even our very lives manifest through four phases. Spring, Summer, Winter, Fall — there are seasons of thought, of growth, of consciousness. Like the four directions, none of the four phases can exist without the others.

Crown (Keter), while it is the Root of all four phases, is not included among them. The reason for this is that Crown plays no part in the actual emanation of the Light. Having no Desire to Receive its power must be activated by the Line. Wisdom, the first extension of the Light, is closely bound up with the Endless in that it exhibits minuscule desire. Each of the subsequent phases is said to become "denser," by virtue of being further removed from the Light, and is hence deemed "lower."

The first three phases, Wisdom, Intelligence, and Beauty, being closely aligned with Crown, all exist in a state of potential until they are revealed through the exertion of this world, Kingdom. While each extension of the Light includes the desire to receive, it is not until the Light reaches the fourth stage Malkhut, that the Light is transformed from a state of potential into a state of revealment when the Desire to Receive is aroused by the emanated.

When the Emanator withdrew so as to create a separation between itself and that which She or He had emanated, residual impressions remained in the Vessels, reminders of their former unity with the Light of Creation. The term "four phases" is generally used to refer to the Light within each of the ten sefirot, whereas the terms, Crown, Wisdom, Intelligence, Beauty, and Kingdom define the impressions or residues of Light which remain in the ten vessels after the Tsimtsum in the World of Restriction.

The elements of what were later to become distinctions in the four phases or grades of will must have existed in the Endless before the Tsimtsum, just as all the various separate nuances of a tree, the leaves, roots, and branches, must exist in the seed, but those differences are undifferentiated and beyond the realm of perception or observance, logic and reason.

Still, we can assume that the emanated, having once known complete and utter fulfillment, must have experienced an understandable lack or deficiency upon separation from the eternal majesty of the Endless Presence. Hence, the first phase of the Light's emanation, Wisdom, might aptly be likened to a child emerging from the womb to find itself in a strange, new environment and experiencing for the first time some sensation of individuation from the mother. Here, in a similar manner as Wisdom is still closely bound up with the Creator, the baby, who is still connected with the mother by the umbilical cord, desires only to be enveloped by and to merge into the arms of the mother, a bond which once secured can never be broken. In subsequent stages of development, as the baby grows into a child, the child into a man or woman, he or she becomes further removed from the parent mentally, emotionally, and physically, yet still continues to feel strong emotional and spiritual ties with the mother — even many years after the mother's finite form, her body, has completed the cycle of its existence.

# 12

## *The Outer Space Connection*

H ERE IN MALKHUT WE ARE PRESENTED WITH ONLY THE
illusionary nature of existence. The real world is hidden. The
Endless Light, *Or En Sof*, all that is, was, or will be, is
present in this world of illusion. The First Three are here —
the Infinite Wisdom is within us and all around us, yet
beyond the scope of our rational senses.

If Reality is here, why do we not experience It?

Kabbalah teaches that the purpose of creation was to
conceal the Infinite to allow us the opportunity of consciously

recreating a circuit of energy through positive resistance and thus removing ourselves from the oppressive energy intelligence which we know as Desire to Receive for Oneself Alone. Although we cannot see reality, taste, touch, hear, or smell it — we can, however, through positive resistance, reveal the Infinite Light and thus alleviate Bread of Shame. Our ability to transcend the illusion and connect with the Infinite, "circular" aspect of existence hinges on a three stage process of *knowing, believing,* and *letting go.*

Knowing makes metaphysical connections. Awareness that there is an alternate, Infinite, universe, here in the same place as this finite world, opens the mind to new possibilities in much the same way as a perceptual connection is made between a climber and the crest of a mountain even before the first step is undertaken. Knowledge, then, is the initial stage in the journey toward transcendence of this negative realm.

Believing that there are Infinitely "higher" and "purer" states of consciousness than those accessible to the mind which accompanies our daily routines, comprises the second level of cosmic awareness. Blind faith is not implied here, but rather a simple emotional experience borne from knowledge and by which one becomes closer to establishing the reality of the higher phases of awareness within one's own consciousness and sub-consciousness.

Letting go, the third and final stage in the journey toward the connection of our "inner space" or consciousness with "outer space", the *Or En Sof* around us, consists of breaking free from the constraints placed upon us by the material illusion. Apprehension often accompanies the introduction of the concept underlying this third stage in the quest for transcendence, for it is often misconstrued as meaning that attachment to the metaphysical realm requires the total abandonment of the physical world, when nothing could be further from the truth. Kabbalah teaches that we can transcend the illusionary physical world entirely and yet still function with elevated efficiency in our daily routines.

In fact, we all disengage from the negative physical world every day and every night of the week — we all meditate; we all transcend the world of illusion; we all experience altered states of consciousness — to not do so would be to court insanity. Music can place us in an altered state; thinking, working, dreaming, daydreaming, even watching television, all of these activities and more can provide us with opportunities for disengagement from this negative realm. The barber who gives a perfectly adequate haircut without any conscious knowledge of having done so, the doctor who correctly diagnosis an illness intuitively without aid from the conscious, rational thought processes, the driver who drives a hundred miles on "automatic pilot," stopping, starting, changing lanes, and finally arrives safely at his destination without the slightest idea of how he got there — all of these are instances of disengagement from the physical world and connection with the metaphysical.

Hence we find that one of the principal differences between the kabbalist and the so-called "average" person who is caught up in the material illusion, is that the kabbalist is conscious of the process of transcendence and is therefore able to use this natural tendency to best advantage whereas the "average" person is not. Whereas the rational pragmatist values highly and struggles always to maintain control of his or her logical, reasoning thought processes, the kabbalist freely abandons analytic sensibility in favor of reaching the higher realms of consciousness which are accessible only by transcending the rational mind.

Another key difference between the rationalist and the kabbalist is that the rationalist mistakenly believes himself to be the instigator of his actions, while the kabbalist, secure in the knowledge that no thought comes about that does not have a preordained solution, sees himself as a channel for energy rather than as a source of it. Having realized that cosmic sentience is Infinitely superior to rational consciousness, and being aware that the only act which can effectively be instigated by humanity is that of positive resistance, the kabbalist initiates situations by which his or her vessel can be used as a conduit for the Infinite power of the *Or En Sof*.

Thus, instead of viewing sojourns into the higher states of awareness as being mere lapses of concentration, and berating him or herself for losing mental control — as does the rational pragmatist — the kabbalist welcomes and initiates opportunities for creative disengagement from the negative illusionary physical world, for by so doing he or she connects with the Infinite.

So conditioned are we to living under the iron hand of the material illusion that today we have come to serve the illusion that poses as reality and to pay tribute to its dominance, praying before the alter of the modern deities, Science and Technology, bowing and scraping as the endless parade of material "progress" marches by. The great paradox and the irony of this age is that the so-called "reality" that we allow to rule us with seeming impunity is really an illusion, and the so-called "fantasy world" — i.e. the thought energy intelligence of dreams, daydreams, and other right-brain activities — so heartily maligned by the self- proclaimed "realists", is the true Reality, the Infinite *Or En Sof*.

Thus we find that the "realists," those who value logic, reason, and common sense above all other human traits and attributes, the "drivers," and the hard-nosed pragmatists, the leaders, and the takers of initiative who mistakenly believe that they are in control of their destinies, are all living in and perpetuating an illusion — while the dreamers, the meditators, the poets, those who spurn the illusion that poses as reality, become, when seen in this new light, the true realists, for they are the ones who are connected to the Infinite Reality of the *Or En Sof*.

Resistance to the material illusion is the key to Reality. Through the three phase process of knowing, believing, and letting go of the material World of Restriction one transcends the illusion and creates a circuit with the alternate universe of the mind, thus becoming a channel for higher states of consciousness. This is true control; this, not the tyranny of the material illusion, is the root of real self-determination and the way by which one transmutes the negative aspect of desire into Desire to Receive for the Sake of Sharing. This, and this alone, is the way one establishes and connects with the Outer Space Connection.

## Ten Not Nine

The word "Sefira" signifies brightness and Infinite luminosity. It refers to Light and vessel together, or, more specifically, Upper Light clothed within a vessel. Yet it is said that no Light illuminates the tenth vessel, Malkhut (Kingdom). How, then, can Kingdom be considered a Sefira in the fullest sense of that word?

The ancient phrase, *Ten, not nine*, refers to this seeming

contradiction in terms. The author of the *Book of Formation* wanted to make it perfectly clear that there are precisely ten and not nine sefirot. Indeed, he went one step further in stating that not only is Kingdom a Sefira, but the most exalted of all of the ten Sefirot.

For reasons well established, the Infinite luminosity contained within Malkhut is concealed. Malkhut is imbued with the same Infinite Upper Light that is embraced within the other nine Sefirot, the only difference being that Malkhut's Endless illumination is revealed only through the restrictive action of the Curtain. The Light repelled by the Curtain, Returning Light, binds with the upper nine Sefirot in the reaction known as Binding by Striking. And so we find that were it not for Malkhut, the Endless Light would have no way of binding with the Upper nine Sefirot, and therefore, because Malkhut demonstrates this unique ability to manifest Upper Light, it must be considered to be the most important Sefira in the Light's revealment.

Thus, there can be no doubt that Malkhut is composed of the Light of the Endless and must therefore be considered a Sefira of the highest order, which clarifies what is meant by the phrase, *Ten, not nine.*

# Part Three

# Expanding Consciousness

# 13

## The Line

THE LINEAR, RATIONAL MIND IS NOT THE REAL MIND, BUT merely a channel, a tool, like a nail that is pounded into a two-by-four. The hammer does not pound the nail. Nothing happens on the physical level without prior activity on the metaphysical plane of thought-consciousness. It is said that the Line is the embodiment of evil which is true from the negative perspective of Malkhut and the lower seven, but from the positive Infinite perspective of the First Three the Line is illusion. The paradox is that the Line, the negative illusion, is our only link with positive reality, the *Or En Sof*.

Illusions are essential impediments to awareness. Words are illusions, but they often tell the truth. Books are illusions — letters, sentences, paragraphs — are channels, nothing more, and yet they have the ability to arouse our curiosity, sharpen our intellects, and more importantly to lead us to a higher state of consciousness and greater awareness of ourselves. Music is illusion, but the emotions that it can arouse are real. Our bodies are illusions in the sense that they reveal nothing of the Infinite Energy-Intelligence within, and yet we are also personifications of Infinity. This whole world is an illusion, and yet it embraces a hidden aspect of reality and it is to this concealed Infinite phase, the First Three, with which it is the kabbalist's task to aspire and to ultimately connect.

The Straight Vessels, the Line, the creative process, came into existence with what, for the sake of utility, is described as being one percent of the Light's capacity. The other ninety-nine percent remains concealed. The one percent is the Line. This phenomenon is demonstrated by the illustration of concentric circles intersected by the Line on page 128. The Line, the one percent, embodies space, time, motion, the Curtain, klippot, the finite body, and all aspects of physical creation. It is the flaw, the gap, the necessary metaphysical distance between the Creator and we the emanated.

We are the Line. Our bodies, these lines of limitation, stand vertical to this sphere, Malkhut. Through resistance we can act as the wire, the filament, the vessel that reveals the *Or En Sof* that of necessity remains concealed, and in so doing we can shed Infinite Light on humanity and also on ourselves.

And herein lies the extent of our free will: We can resist and act as channels to the higher realms of awareness or not resist and remain in darkness as we so desire. The Line, then, is the bane of humanity, but also our only source of beauty, for it is solely through the resistance intrinsic to the limited aspect of the Line that we can absolve Bread of Shame.

## The Lights of Life and Spirit

The Light of the Line was deemed by the Ari to be superior to the Light of the Circles. This may seem odd in view of the fact that the Light of the Circles was the source from which everything, including the illusionary Light of the Line originated. However, the Ari, in his abundant wisdom, realized that as the Circles receive their re-illumination solely from the Light of the Line, thus, from our finite perspective, it is the Light of the Line that must be considered by far the more important.

Indeed, were it not for the Light of the Line, the Infinite Circular Vessels would never be "drawn down" or "extend" from the Endless and thus would never be revealed. When viewed from this perspective it becomes readily apparent why the Ari felt obliged to make this important distinction.

The Ari called the Light of the Line, "Light of Spirit," while to the Light of the Circles he gave the name, "Light of Nefesh." In Hebrew the word, *nefesh*, meaning "crude spirit," was also applied by the Ari in describing the latter circular Light, indicating the infinite Light's lesser importance to this world.

The lower seven of the Line serve as initiators in the process of the revealment of Light in the Circles. The Crown (Keter) of Circles must be illuminated before the Wisdom (Hokhmah) of Circles can receive illumination, the Wisdom of

Circles must be revealed before Understanding (Binah) of Circles can be re-illuminated, and so on. However, the Circular vessels themselves are totally incapable of their own revelation. The Light of the Circles is revealed only when acted upon by the Light of the Line.

The Line, in other words, triggers all revelation in the circular vessels. And as the Light of the Line (Light of the Spirit) always precedes the Light of the Circles (Light of Nefesh — Crude Spirit), at least from the finite perspective, the Light of the Line was considered by the Ari, Isaac Luria to be superior to the Light of the Circles.

When we the vessels refused to accept the Light's blessing and beseeched the Creator for a way by which to relieve Bread of Shame, the Creator withdrew the Light's Infinite blessing and thus granted to man a form of equivalence with the Light. And so it is that since the Tsimstum the creator in this finite world is man.

So while it is true that the Circles are the epitome of infinite perfection, whereas the Line is finite, hence flawed, still we owe our entire physical existence to the Line. Were it not for the Line we would have no corporeal essence, no Desire to Receive, for oneself alone, no way of relieving Bread of Shame, and consequently no means by which to complete our Tikune, the soul's period of correction. With this in mind, it becomes a simple matter to understand why the Light of the Spirit is considered more important than the Light of Nefesh.

**The Line Connects the Circles**

All manifestations physical and metaphysical advance

through four phases each of which is comprised of ten sefirot. There is, however, an aspect of negativity in the finite, linear aspect of creation (the Line) caused by Mesach (the Curtain) which imparts the illusion of darkness to the lower seven of the Line. This negative facet is transposed to the Circles, giving them the illusion of having the same deficiency as that which is manifested by the Line. The reason for this, as has been explained, is that the Circles receive all of their renewed Illumination solely through the Line. Thus, we find that while the Circles are eternal and utterly devoid of space or illusion, both the Line and the Circle appear from our limited perspective to possess the same imperfection.

Given the illusion of darkness present in the lower seven of the Line, one might conclude that the Line is incapable of reactivating the Light that is held in suspended animation within the Encircling vessels, but that would be an erroneous assumption. Each phase requires a full aggregate of ten sefirot for its revealment, and the Line of Keter (also called the Ten Sefirot of Primordial Man) is the only method by which this re-illumination can be accomplished. Therefore the lower seven sefirot of the Line can and must link, bind, and re-illuminate the Ten Sefirot in each of the upper first three Sefirot of the line which connect with the Ten Sefirot of each Circular Sefira.

Wisdom must be fully activated before the next phase, Intelligence, can be revealed, Intelligence must be restored to its former Infinite splendor before Beauty can manifest, and all ten vessels of Beauty must be animated before Kingdom can be activated.

The following diagram will help to clarify the method by which this is accomplished.

Illustration of concentric circles with rays of Light separating in V formations.

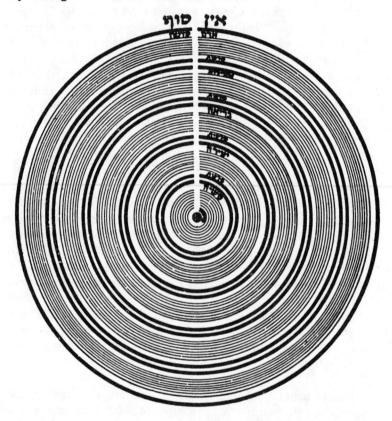

Notice that at each of the four phases of Circles — each of which is comprised of ten sefirot — the majority of Light is repelled by the Curtain. The First Three (Keter, Hokhmah, Binah) of each phase of the Line enters each phase of the Circles in a potential state. Not until the Light touches the

Curtain of each phase are the ten sefirot of each corresponding phase re-illuminated — i.e. the First Three of the phase of Wisdom in the Line re-illuminates all ten sefirot in the Circular phase of Wisdom before the Light passes downward to the next phase. The Light reflected by the Curtain in each phase then descends through the seven lower sefirot of each phase, after which the First Three of the next phase strikes the Curtain of the lower phase and the same process is repeated.

The resistance of the Curtain which is located after the Head (the First Three) but before the Body (the lower seven) of each phase (in other words between Binah and Tiferet) represents the casting off Bread of Shame which not only sheds Illumination outward and upward but also allows the Light's blessing to descend to the next lower level.

The Light is greatly diffused by each subsequent phase. This action can aptly be likened to the repulsion and diffusion of sunlight in the various layers of Earth's atmosphere, each of which reflects much of the light while allowing an ever decreasing quantity of the light's full spectrum to descend to Earth.

Please note that the above example, as with all physical comparisons, should not be taken entirely at face value. The student should be ever watchful of literal interpretations of kabbalistic material. Physical comparisons such as the one given above can be misleading. The phenomenon of which we are speaking occurs also on the metaphysical or potential level through the phases of Crown, Wisdom, Intelligence, and Beauty. Only when the Light reaches the Curtain of Malkhut (Kingdom) — where Desire to Receive for Oneself Alone (which itself is analogous to the Earth's gravity) is fully aroused — does the Endless Light become exposed on the level of physical actuality and, at last, is the true purpose of creation revealed.

Although correct from an "objective" point of view (perhaps "rational" is a better word, true objectivity being humanly impossible) the above example is not indicative of the entire process as described by Kabbalah. The teachings of Kabbalah must be viewed from various angles to be fully comprehended. So while we find that the above comparisons hold true on their intended physical (sunlight) and metaphysical (spiritual/thought) levels, it is of utmost importance to consider this four phase process of Illumination also from a personal perspective. In other words, the Illumination of which we are speaking is both "physical" as in the revealment of sunlight and "metaphysical" as it relates to the potential and thought realms, however it must never be forgotten that when the kabbalist speaks of Malkhut he is also referring to the heart of man.

Let us, then, summarize the method by which the Light descends through the four phases. The Head of the Line enters the Circle of Keter. The Light strikes the Curtain and much of the Light is repelled. The resistant action of the Curtain (Binding by Striking) allows the First Three of the Line to Illuminate all ten sefirot of Keter of the Circles and also allows a lesser amount of Light to be drawn downward. The diffused Light descends, passing through the lower seven straight sefirot of Crown and down through the First Three of the next phase, Hokhmah, where it strikes the Curtain of that phase and the process is repeated.

Remember that the Light must pass through the lower seven sefirot of each phase before the ten sefirot of the phase

below can be manifested. Thus do the lower seven in the
Line, though unrevealed themselves, still accomplish the
unification of the Ten Upper Circular Sefirot with the Ten
Sefirot in the lower ten Circular Sefirot of each phase and
descend to each subsequent phase below.

**Here and Now**

The Ari, Rabbi Luria took great pains to be certain that
his students understood that *all* phases of existence are
connected by the Line which extends from the Endless. He
explained in fine detail how the Light is drawn down through
one circle after another until all of the phases have been
perfected and completed. He caused his students to examine
thoroughly the exact method by which Light descends
through one layer to the next, becoming more and more
concealed until, at last, by the time it arrives at this lowest
level, Malkhut, It is almost totally devoid of revealed
Illumination. Rabbi Luria was most meticulous, too, in his
explanation of the process by which the Curtain, through
involuntary resistance, allows all of the three previous phases,
plus Malkhut, the phase of revealment, to become animated,
but how we, the emanated, can attain contentment only
through conscious restriction. Why should the Ari have
considered it important to place so much emphasis on that
which to some might seem at first glance to be picayune
technicalities?

The Ari was imparting to us what might be described as
the "pantheistic" perspective of Kabbalah which posits that the
Force, the Light, pierces each and every stratum of existence,
that the Emanator is all-embracing, that every molecule,
atom, and sub-atomic particle in the universe is imbued with
the power of the *Or En Sof* — that the Creator is within us
and

without us, a part of us, yet apart from us, and that everything in the universe is but an aspect of one, living, breathing organism.

Some spiritual teachings place the Creator high on a lofty ethereal pedestal, far beyond the reach of humanity. In some religions it becomes necessary to die in order to "meet your Maker." Other philosophies see the Emanator as having created the universe before moving on to bigger and presumably better things. By his thorough teaching the Ari was attempting to clarify the kabbalistic concept that the En Sof permeates every aspect of the universe and that this is true no matter how concealed, from our limited perspective, the Light may seem to appear.

We will learn in due time how each subsequent phase conceals the one that emerged previously. One of the many analogies drawn by the Ari explains this phenomenon in terms of the various layers of an onion, each of which tastes the same. Using this metaphor for the purpose of understanding the all-pervasiveness of the Light, Rabbi Luria pointed out that just as the essence, the taste, of the onion is the same throughout all of its layers, so too does the Light, the essence of existence, permeate every aspect of material substance as well as the intangible aspects of existence with equal consistency.

The onion metaphor serves, also, as an apt illustration of what is meant, kabbalistically, by the terms higher and lower in the sense that the inner layers are no lower or less real than the outer covering, but only more concealed. So we find that while one level of consciousness may be higher than the next, in essence they are all identical. The only difference between Hokhmah, the highest phase, and Malkhut, the lowest, is in the degree of revealment, Hokhmah being revealed, Malkhut, concealed, but in fact they both consist of the same *Or En Sof*.

Another example used by the Ari was that of a lantern covered with layer after layer of thin fabric veils, each of which conceals the light still further. Imagine a scenario in which one person enters a room at the moment when another is placing the last of one hundred veils over a lantern. The lantern is there beneath the veils and its light is still as bright as ever, but the new observer sees no lantern and thus quite naturally, though mistakenly, concludes that the first person has before him nothing more than a pile of cloth. Such is the prevailing condition here in Malkhut as it relates to the *Or En Sof*.

The Creator is here, the sages, the saints. The Upper worlds are here along with the Lower. The negative is entwined with the positive, the high with the low, the dense with the fine, the good with the bad. The Light is here in all of its Infinite glory, but it must remain hidden from our finite aspect, the lower seven, for that was the prerequisite of our existence. Reality is here and now, within us and without us, but concealed by the space, the gap, the illusion, that was the sole imperative of creation.

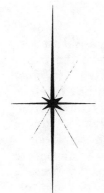

# 14

## *On Restoring Light to the Circles*

Aᴛᴀᴇ ᴛᴀᴇ ᴛꜱɪᴍᴛꜱᴜᴍ, ᴀ ɴᴇɢᴀᴛɪᴠᴇ ꜱᴘᴀᴄᴇ ᴡᴀꜱ established in the Circles by the lower seven of the Line. Thus, from Keter to Hokhmah there is a gap of seven empty stages; from Hokhmah to Binah another gap of seven, and so on. Each of these negative spaces is an outgrowth of the illusionary process of Line. The First Three of each phase of the Line can fill the ten sefirot of each phase of the Circles, but the lower seven of the Line do not have that ability. The Ari's book of meditations describes a specific method by which prayer can fill the gaps and restore Light to the circular vessels.

Just as the energy of the seed must first establish itself as a root before a trunk can come into being, and the trunk before the branch, and the branch before the leaf, so must the Light travel through the lower seven of each phase before it can illuminate the adjacent level below. The Light, in other words, must pass through the lower seven straight sefirot of Keter before Hokhmah's Light of Wisdom can manifest; it must then pass through the lower seven of Hokhmah before Binah's Light of Mercy can be revealed. The same process is maintained throughout the ten levels of all four phases.

In our examination of the filament of a light bulb, we learned that it is the filament's negative restriction that is responsible for the Light's revealment. So too, in this world of illusion, does the Light require Malkhut's resistance to reveal Its supremely positive blessing. At all phases it is the level of Malkhut that causes the Light's re-illumination. Malkhut has the unique ability of manifesting the Light. She alone possesses Desire to Receive for the Self Alone and hence the restrictive capacity requisite for the Light's revealment. Only within the tenth and final sefirot of each phase, Malkhut, does the restriction occur which provides the stimulus for the revelation of Light in each subsequent phase.

No evolution or revealment occurs in the lower phases, even in the circular vessels, unless and until there is a manifestation of the seven straight line sefirot of the phase above. The seven lower straight sefirot of Keter link the ten circular sefirot of Keter with the ten Circular sefirot of Hohkmah, and so from Hokhmah to Binah, and so on in a like manner. The circular vessels of Hokhmah, for example, receive illumination from the First Three of the Line of Hokhmah; while the circular vessels of Binah receive their illumination from the First Three of the Line of Binah. This is what the Ari meant when he declared that the lower seven sefirot of straightness unify all of the Circular Vessels by virtue of the Line.

It may strike the reader as a discrepancy that the infinitely positive Light, the essence of Reality, requires negative illusion for its revealment. After all, did the Ari not teach us that Light is infinitely superior to and always supersedes darkness? Adding to this seeming contradiction is the fact that the Ari also taught us that no positive energy is revealed in this illusionary world without resistance, the energy-intelligence of which is inherently negative. No light, sound, thought, word, deed — nothing is revealed in this world of illusion without resistance. Positive cannot be revealed without negative, the Light needs the darkness. Such is the nature of the paradox of Returning Light. How, then, can we harmonize these seeming contradictions?

Because the Light requires negative resistance to be revealed in this world should not be construed as meaning that the Emanator's beneficence is in some way limited by the vessel. Like sunlight, the Light's beneficence is constant. Would it not be a mistake to say that the sunlight ceases to shine during the nighttime hours just because the dark side of the earth happens for the moment to be facing away from the sun? Like the sunlight, the Light, *Or En Sof*, gives of its endless beneficence twenty-four hours of every day. That fact that we may not see the Light does not mean It is not within us and without us, endlessly sharing Its infinite abundance.

From the Infinite perspective darkness does not exist. The Light, *Or En Sof*, is everywhere, constantly imparting Its endless blessing. It is only from our finite point of view that the Light appears to be concealed. This was a prerequisite of creation in that it provides us with a way of earning the Light's blessing and thus removing Bread of Shame.

The Ari's example, mentioned earlier, involving the removal of the veils covering a lantern may help to clarify this matter. The light beneath the layers of veils never ceased to shine, but from the perspective of one who might have walked into the room at the time when the veils covered the lantern, the light would have seemed to not exist. So it is with the infinite Light of our beings. We must use voluntary resistance to remove the veils of illusion from the lower seven and thus again reveal the endless illumination of our circular vessels. Restriction, the removal of the veils, reveals Light in the lower seven of the Line. By injecting restriction we transform the illusionary phase of the seven and change the darkness into Light.

The seven of Keter create an illusionary gap, as do the seven of Hokhmah, and the seven of Binah, and so on. Thus the seven of each phase remain dark and unrevealed. However, as strange as it may seem, the Ari taught us that even though the seven may seem totally devoid of Light, whereas the First Three of the phase below are illuminated, the seven in the higher phase are considered to be more exalted. The seven of the phase above, in other words, are deemed superior to the First Three of the phase below because they are found in a higher frame of reference.

If Light is superior to darkness, does it not stand to reason that the Light found in the First Three of the phase below should be superior to the darkness of the phase above? Have we not been told that Light always prevails over darkness? Why then should the Illumination found in the First Three of the lower phase not be judged superior to the seven of the phase above which is cloaked in darkness?

The reason that this was not seen by the Ari as being a inconsistency was that the darkness found in the lower seven is an illusion. The Light is there in all of it's infinite glory, but obscured from our "view" here in the illusionary realm. Thus the Light in the seven of the upper phases, though veiled, is still closer to the source and must thus be deemed purer and higher by virtue of its closer proximity to the Endless.

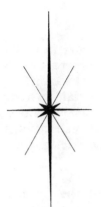

# 15

## *Activating*
## *The Central Column*

THE UNIVERSE OPERATES ON A THREE COLUMN SYSTEM. Acting between the positive influence and the negative is the mediating principle known to Kabbalah as the Central Column. The Central Column is synonymous with the neutron in the atom and also with the filament in a light bulb. The Central Column represents the mediating principle which must bridge the two polarities, positive and negative, in order that energy can be manifested.

The Central Column can be likened to the moderator in a debate, a referee, a diplomat, or the arbitrator of any dispute.

Just as the filament must exercise resistance in order to reveal light, so too must the arbitrator restrain his own particular opinions or beliefs in the interest of settling the conflict, whatever it may be. Like the intermediary, we all want to have our way, to receive, in other words, for ourselves alone. The paradox is that to accomplish this we must restrict what we want to receive, for it is only through restriction that energy is revealed.

Restriction is the energy-intelligence of the Central Column. By resisting what we want to receive we create the connection that gives it to us. How strange this concept seems at first glance, how backward, how thoroughly wrong-headed. Can the kabbalist seriously expect us to believe that to get what we want we have to reject it? — that to arrive at yes we have to say no? Yes, as strange as it may seem, the principle of Returning Light dictates a situation such, that all energy that is revealed in this world of restriction is reflected (restricted) energy. Hence, if we want to receive (in other words reveal the energy we desire) we have to withhold our desire and thereby create a blockage to the actual receiving. The moment we say no the Central Column creates interference in the world of Malkhut which allows the Light, the positive energy, to be revealed.

**Resistance**

Students of Kabbalah generally have no difficulty understanding how the negative pole's resistance to the incoming electricity initiates illumination in a light bulb. Nor do they have the slightest problem understanding the concept of resistance when confronted with some of the myriad physical examples of this phenomenon in action. All one has to do is contract a muscle (resistance) to see that it grows. Compare a reflective light-colored surface with an absorbent darker-colored one in strong sunlight — there is no question that the former sheds (resists) more illumination than the latter. By clashing one rock forcibly against another the concept of Binding by Striking flashes to life before our eyes. Yet, however easily one may accept physical examples of resistance (Curtain) and restriction (Tsimtsum) in exterior terms, still we struggle when attempting to apply this concept to our daily lives.

Modern nations, cultures and civilizations, were founded and built, we are told, by men and women who believed in a philosophy of setting goals and striving toward them. Every day in school, on television, in books and magazines, we are presented with examples of people who through their apparent dogged striving have "made something of themselves." When at first we don't succeed, the prevailing wisdom goes, try, try again. It is little wonder, then, that when the kabbalist attempts to inform us that the greater is our desire to possess something the less likely will be our chance of acquiring it, and, conversely, that resisting that which we most desire is the surest way of getting it; our personalities — that body of knowledge perceived by the senses and learned from birth —cry out in protest. This seeming contradiction rubs against the grain of all that we have ever learned. How are we expected to "get somewhere in this world" if we reject that which we most desire?

It is one thing, after all, to look at physical examples of resistance in action, and quite another to adopt it as a way of life. One important obstacle to contend with is the bias of Newtonian physics. Newton believed that nature is governed by absolute laws which operate totally apart from the consciousness of man. The Newtonian perspective, acquired by all who attend our schools, conditions us to believe that we can study nature without considering ourselves as part of the equation. So seemingly universal is this misconception that it is generally accepted without question.

Kabbalah, on the other hand, teaches that man is a participator in nature and therefore cannot possibly study its laws without also studying himself. Hence, the kabbalist merely by observing the laws that govern the external physical world — such as Binding by Striking — concludes that the same laws must also be acting internally within each of us. Resistance, then, being the modus operandi in the physical world, must also rule the realm of the metaphysical, including our emotional lives and even our thoughts. As basic and utterly sensible as this idea "feels" when it is expressed in simple terms, it still escapes the vast majority of people — expressly for the reason stated earlier that most people perceive nature as something apart from themselves.

Given these prevailing cultural perspectives and educational conditions, it is little wonder that the student of Kabbalah cannot grasp, at first, and therefore will not embrace wholeheartedly the concept of resistance. It is not easy, after all, to break the bonds of teachings so deeply ingrained. The verity of resistance, this most elusive element of kabbalistic thought, must be approached from various levels and angles, mentally, emotionally, and physically if it is to be fully comprehended and utilized to best advantage. As is the case with all kabbalistic truths, the idea of resisting that which is most desired cannot be perceived by means of logic alone — it must be experienced. Rational thinking is a tool, but like any tool it has its limitations.

Concerning this seemingly enigmatic kabbalistic concept, it should be remembered that it is not the Light that the kabbalist asks us to reject, but the obstruction of Light, the Desire to Receive for Oneself Alone. By resisting that which we most desire we create an altered state of consciousness, which though admittedly paradoxical from the standpoint of logic and common sense (as those words are commonly perceived), satisfies all desires. Self depravation plays not the slightest part in the kabbalist's resistance and denial. It is simply that by reenacting Tsimtsum, the original act of creation, he or she creates affinity with the Light and achieves union with the *Or En Sof*.

**The Filament**

In our discussion of the filament of a light bulb we learned that the negative pole and not the positive initiates any and all circuits of energy. The Line makes contact with the Circle thereby creating the circular condition necessary for the Light's revealment. The resulting circuit satisfies both the desire of the Line, to receive, as well as that of the Circles which is to share.

The brightness of a light bulb is determined solely by the size of the filament, not by the current that runs through the wiring system. The current is the same no matter what appliance is plugged into it, whether it is an air conditioner, the demands of which are great, or a five watt bulb, the desire of which is small. In a similar manner as a light bulb produces only that amount of light which its filament is capable of generating, so too can we manifest only that exact amount of Light which our filament (our capacity for restriction) allows our inner Encircling Vessels to reveal.

**Returning Light**

Lurianic Kabbalah classifies Light according to two
divisions, Straight Light and Returning Light. From the
human perspective the latter is by far the more important.
This becomes apparent by simply examining these two aspects
of Light relative to the physical universe. Straight Light
becomes manifested only upon contact with resistance.
Sunlight, the corporeal equivalent of Straight Light, is
revealed only when it reflects off something physical —
evidence of which is readily available by gazing into the night
sky where no light is manifested between the planetary
bodies. The light that is reflected is given the name Returning
Light. Hence, because Straight Light is invisible the greater
importance of Returning Light over Straight Light is
indisputable, insofar as we of Malkhut are concerned, for the
simple reason that Returning Light is the only light that is
revealed and is thus the only light we ever see.

Because non-reflected light is not physically manifested is
not proof that it does not exist. Light is everywhere, in the
air, the water, and even in the center of the Earth. The
Infinite presence of the *Or En Sof* permeates that which is
physical and that which is immaterial with equal intensity, as
does the light of the sun. The paradox is that no light is
revealed unless by an act of resistance. And therein lies the
essential difference between Straight Light and Returning
Light, the latter reveals everything, the former, nothing.

An earlier chapter advanced what to the rational mind
might seem like a ludicrous notion, namely that every wish is
potentially granted, every desire is already fulfilled. From the
kabbalistic perspective this concept makes perfect sense, for
no desire can possibly arise, the fulfillment of which has not

been attained on a metaphysical level. Nothing is manifested in this World of Restriction without there having existed a previous thought for the simple reason that nothing, but nothing, exists today that did not exist in the En Sof before the Thought of Creation — no thought, no deed, no aspiration or Desire.

Recall that the greater the capacity for reflection (resistance) the greater is the revealment of light. A white surface, for example, reflects more light than a dark one, a hard, shiny object such as a mirror more than a porous object such as a rock — which is precisely why Desire to Receive for Oneself Alone, being the epitome of absorbency, reveals nothing, while the Desire to Receive for the Sake of Sharing, being of a reflective nature, reveals all that can be revealed. The same holds true on the levels of the metaphysical, and even, as we shall now examine, on the most mundane levels of human experience.

What follows are a few examples of how the concept of Returning Light might apply to our everyday lives.

Two businessmen shake hands, one offering a firm grip and a smile, the other a passive grip with no facial expression.

Result: No deal.

Union demands new contract, management stalls.

Result: Strike.

Mother serves sumptuous meal to unappreciative children.

Result: TV dinners.

Professor tutors student who does not listen.

Result: The purpose of both is defeated.

Wife attempts to communicate, but husband watches football on TV.

Result: Husband loses TV in divorce settlement.

Conscious restriction is not required on the part of the earth, the moon, or other planetary objects in order to reflect the light of the sun. Nor is a body of water or any other physical object compelled to voluntarily reflect sunlight in order the light may be revealed. Light reflects from a mirror without the mirror's conscious intervention. The filament repels electricity with no act of awareness. Only humanity must exercise voluntary resistance to reveal Light. Failure to restrict or otherwise reflect the Light which is freely offered can result in enmity, financial disaster, lack of order and communication, obesity, alcoholism, and a host of other problems, whereas voluntarily resistance allows us to fulfill our true purpose which is to achieve affinity with the Light through the removal of Bread of Shame.

### Free Will or Determinism

Free will is a privilege reserved only for those who choose to exercise it. The Ari taught us that the extent of man's free will rests in his ability and willingness to restrict the negative aspect of desire. Either we resist the Desire to Receive for the Self Alone and thus reveal the Light that lies dormant within us, or we do not restrict and remain submerged in the illusion. Failure to engage the system of restriction that grants us free will causes us to be ruled by the same deterministic system that causes a rock to fall to the ground or a planet to revolve around the sun.

A rock has no free will. Nor does a man who does not exercise resistance against the Desire to Receive for the Self alone. Consciousness requires a ceaseless effort at resistance. By choosing not to restrict the negative aspect of desire we give up the one prerogative that was granted to us after the Tsimtsum, namely, the right to alleviate Bread of Shame. By restricting the negative aspect of desire we pay tribute to that original act of creation and thus reveal the Light.

# 16

## *The Good Fight*

MERELY TO LIST, LET ALONE RECOUNT, ALL OF THE atrocities committed by men and women in the name of "goodness," "truth," and "righteousness" would require a million megabytes of computer memory. All wars, all battles, are fought, supposedly, with the intention of eradicating some evil, righting some real or imagined wrong. This continuing cycle of violence in the name of high virtue has been with us since the earliest days of civilization and it will no doubt continue for some time to come.

Hypothetically, violence might be justified, from the

kabbalistic perspective, in the unlikely event that the combatants were attempting to create affinity with the Light and thus restore the Circular integrity of humanity and all that exists on this planet. That would be a good fight, a fight worth winning, a fight worth "dying" for. Of course no one fights to preserve the Circular aspect of humanity. In truth, the vast majority of wars, battles, and arguments, are fought by combatants who desire nothing more than to safeguard their own selfish self interests.

Politicians and world leaders may pay lip service to such concepts as world peace, but in the final analysis, when push comes to shove, almost invariably their true colors show through the veneer of illusion by which they surround themselves, and we see that greed, Desire to Receive for Oneself Alone, is their real motivating factor.

In short, they are fighting to preserve an illusion. Neck hairs bristle when this kabbalistic concept is expressed, throats are cleared, blood comes to faces — egos get fighting mad. All of us have known people, good people, loved ones, who have died protecting what the kabbalist so glibly, it seems, calls an illusion. What of World War Two — was that not a classic example of a good fight of truth conquering evil? Who among us does not cherish the memory of someone, a family member, a compatriot or loved one, who died protecting a beloved homeland or way of life? Does the kabbalist have the temerity to suggest that all of those precious lives were sacrificed in vain?

Naturally, from that standpoint of reasoning, anyone who is not ready to shed his or her blood, or better yet the blood of others, to protect their "God-given" homelands and cherished ways of life is, at best, a coward. It is precisely this

mentality that sends young men off to war. Only later, when
the war is over and carnage is complete and the battlefields
are strewn with blood and body parts, and nothing, but
*nothing* has been accomplished, do a few people raise their
voices to decry the utter futility of it all — and perhaps for a
brief moment someone hears those voices before the cycle of
violence begins anew.

War is an aspect of the Line, and therefore,
kabbalistically speaking, illusionary. In the grand Circular
scheme of things there is no difference between Arab and
Jew, Negro and Caucasian, Catholic and Protestant — these
differences are temporal in the sense that we possess them
only for the speck of "time" which each of our finite lives
encompasses.

Yet, in spite of war's illusionary nature, the kabbalist
does not contend that those who die in war necessarily do so
in vain. War is an illusion — make no mistake about that.
Still, as are all aspects of this illusionary finite existence, it
can also be an opportunity for correction — not religious,
political, or planetary correction (in that respect wars solve
nothing) — but personal, karmic correction.

Consider, then, the possibility that our beloved ancestors
who sacrificed their finite vessels in war, did not do so in
defence of imagined differences and false beliefs. Perhaps
they were motivated by a purpose higher than the mere
preservation of some illusionary doctrine, religion, or the
"ownership" of some piece of ground. Perhaps they died,
rather, to complete a phase of their spiritual correction. Using
this reasoning we find that even war, man's most senseless
and futile illusionary gesture, can be resolved within the
Infinite Circular perspective.

## The Global Village

Only recently has the concept of world citizenship reached the feathered edge of the collective consciousness. Today many people, if pressed for an opinion, would agree, at least in principle, with the concept that the world might be a better place if it were governed by a single international ruling body. Yet, as with so many altruistically motivated ideas, few people, no matter how humanitarian their intentions, can agree even on what such a forum might realistically accomplish, much less on how a plan of this nature might be implemented.

If such a body politic existed, how would it function?

Some see the world government as being an outgrowth of the United Nations. The current organization, they maintain, could be expanded to include all of the world's nations and territories, and U.N. decrees, instead of being elective, would become mandatory. Certain economists, on the other hand, contend that only free enterprise could be the catalyst for such a plan. If all of the world's economies were inextricably bound up with one another, they reason, there would be far less incentive for one country to wage war against another. Many military men insist that a strong nuclear arsenal is the way to bring peace to the world. The threat of nuclear carnage, they tell us, is the only reason we are not at war today. Certain evangelists agree, insisting that only religion — meaning the fear of God — coupled with a fearsome nuclear retaliatory capability, can save the world.

Of course, there is a large contingency of detractors who maintain that nothing short of an all-out invasion from outer space could possibly bring all of the nations and the people of the world together. Even this argument is not without merit. Indeed, given the current state of world affairs, it is difficult to imagine five human beings coexisting peaceably, let alone five or more billion.

Those who vehemently oppose the idea of a unified world government point to the dullness of a homogenized world in which everyone would be the same. Detractors argue that cultural identities would be lost, racial and religious distinctions obliterated, and we would be left with the blandness of a vast, homogenized cultural wasteland. And, certainly, this argument, too, warrents consideration — at least from the point of view of those who believe it to be true.

The point is that even among those who doubtlessly agree with the basic concept of a single international ruling body, no one has yet to, or is likely to, it seems, given prevailing world tensions, advance a formula as to how such a scheme might plausibly be brought into being. It seems that an almost insurmountable obstacle faces the idea of a One World government. For such a forum to be effective, a quality would have to be exercised rarely found in human interactions, namely, selflessness. This fact leads many people, even supporters of the One World cause, to conclude that the idea of a united world is doomed to failure.

Not so the kabbalist.

Kabbalists have long maintained that world unity will one day be a physical reality. It is the kabbalist's belief that a millennium of world peace will precede the final emendation. Even here, today, in this chaotic riot of insanity which we mistakenly call the real world, the careful observer can perceive the emergence of a seed of changing awareness in this transitional period in humanity's tumultuous, yet curiously static, cultural evolution. The very fact that certain people are thinking, speaking, even raising their voices in behalf of One World is evidence of the vast, sweeping reformation that is to come. As always, the metaphysical realm of thought is the harbinger of what will one day become reality on the physical level.

In Reality, meaning the Infinite reality of the *Or En Sof*, we are all cut from the same cloth. Each of us holds a share in a common stock, a stock which might be aptly named, Survival International — and the price of that stock is rising daily. In terms of the Endless Reality. The Infinite recognizes no distinction between the weak and the strong, poor and rich, Arab and Jew, commoner and king. In the grand scheme of things, we are already intimately entwined within a vast, never-changing fabric of universal peace.

Assuredly, here in this fourth phase of existence, the fighting continues, the torture, the selfishness, the seemingly perpetual bickering, but this is of circumstance only in the transitory world, the World of Illusion. Outward appearances only appear to make us different; customs and languages only *seem* to separate us. Kabbalists see cultures, races, religions, and political movements as being of consequence only in the illusory world — hence of no consequence at all. These ephemeral distinctions play not the slightest part in the great, unchanging and ever-peaceful design.

All that exists within a life cycle having a beginning, middle, and an end, is considered by the Kabbalah to be part of the illusion. Physical differences, being of a finite nature, are illusionary. Our bodies, these vessels of limitation, with which we maneuver through the various phases of the earthly cycle of correction, are here today and gone tomorrow, and hence must also be considered illusion.

Kabbalistically speaking, only that which is permanent and never-changing is real. Nothing ever changes in the *Or En Sof*. It is Endless, and, as such, it was, is, and forever will be endlessly peaceful, timeless, and perfectly still. Our souls live forever as part of the endless circle of infinity — thus, only they, of all human attributes and characteristics, are deemed by Kabbalah to be bona fide expressions of Reality.

Admittedly, the possibility of all of the world's politicians, economists, religious and military leaders suddenly agreeing to abide by the dictates of a single international ruling body, seems, from the finite perspective, to be remote in the extreme. However, still and all, from the Infinite point of view, those who aspire toward a One World government have just cause for celebration. For whether they know it or not, their wish has already been granted. From the Infinite outlook, the universe and everything in it has always been and will always be a single unified entity.

The world is One.

In the real, the Endless world, peace already reigns supreme. As difficult as it may be to imagine, experiencing as we do only the underside of reality, it is just a matter of time (another illusory concept) before the aspiration for a united world becomes reality here in the World of Illusion.

Even today, the world operates under the auspices of a single authority, a unified Energy-Intelligence, the name of which is *Or En Sof*. Even in this violent, transitory, tumultuous sphere of illusion there is an all-embracing aspect of harmony, peace, and unanimity with which each of us can connect. Thus, when seen from the kabbalistic point of view, the concept of a global village, as expressed by the late visionary and architect, R. Buckminster Fuller, becomes not some tangled, international impossibility, but an intimate matter of personal choice and individual commitment.

# 17

## *Tikune, Zaddik,*
## *Coming Full Circle*

HROUGHOUT THE AGES WRITERS, PHYSICIANS, AND
metaphysicians have been holding out to us the tantalizing
proposition that a medicinal formula might one day be
discovered that will once and for all put an end to human
suffering. Alchemists searched for centuries for an elixir that
would give us all eternal youth. Theirs and other utopian
worlds of the imagination have played a large part in the
continuing drama of the human psyche for they offer hope of
a better world. Aldous Huxley imagined such a panacea in his
novel *Brave New World*. Many have dreamed of such a world,
but from the kabbalistic perspective the discovery of a

panacea that would end all human suffering would result in a human tragedy of unparalleled magnitude, in some ways worse than all wars, famines, epidemics, and atrocities combined.

What reason could the kabbalist possibly have for making this seeming outlandish declaration? Is it that the world population would skyrocket to such an extent that people would be fighting over every scrap of food? No, that problem could easily be alleviated simply by switching to a vegetarian diet. Cattle require an inordinate amount of grazing land that could be utilized in more productive ways. Nor does strange assertion have anything to do with either the problem of overcrowding or with energy. Solar, wind, wave energy, and other alternative sources could be employed to fill energy needs, and even today it is within the range of possibility that undersea or space stations could be developed to handle excess population. The real grounds for the kabbalists opinion that a life-extending elixir would result in a major disaster is precisely for the reason that it would end all earthly suffering which would only serve to prolong the spiritual suffering of humanity, thus extending our *Tikune*, the corrective process.

We are here to make adjustments, corrections, amendments to our finite constitutions, and these changes come about through resistance, discomfort and suffering. Each lifetime brings us closer to our goal of one day being reunited with the great Circle of Endlessness from which we came. This corrective procedure is called *Tikune*. The Line, the creative illusion, the lower seven of the Line, are all names for the same process of spiritual modification. Finite existence, this life in the lower seven, provides us with the opportunity of expelling Bread of Shame. Through resistance the soul is purified, bringing us closer to the Circle of beneficence that is the birthright of us all. Thus it becomes apparent why a magical panacea that would remove all suffering would turn the human drama into a tragedy for the simple reason that it would only prolong the agony of finite existence.

Our souls are like streams that can never rest until they once again mingle with the Infinite sea. Until that time comes we meander, trying out new channels, new lines of least resistance. Sometimes the stream of life swells and rises, sometimes it cascades down like a waterfall. At times the water is shallow at other times deep, sometimes dark and murky, sometimes pure and crystal clear. At times we enter lakes of the spirit that are so large and still that they deceive us into thinking that we have reached the ocean of endlessness that we have sought so long. Sometimes we are lured by gravity into swamps of uncertainty, sometimes we are trapped in tidal pools from which we fear we might never escape. From lifetime to lifetime the stream goes on, searching, suffering, pursuing the Infinite reunion.

We each have but one true aspiration and that is to return to the Light, the same Light that once filled us in the En Sof before the Thought of Creation, the same Light that left its impression in our Encircling Vessels. Life, this finite existence is a line, a channel, a stream, that was once a part of the great Circle of Infinity and to the Circle it will one day return. And so while it is true that from our finite perspective, suffering has nothing whatever to recommend it, and thus a magical life-extending elixir would seem like a glorious blessing. But, from the Infinite point of view we see that suffering is a necessity, for it is only through the process of correction, Tikune, that we can ever return home to the state of blissful beneficence from which the stream of life originated.

### The Mother of Invention

Consider a hypothetical situation in which an intrepid sea captain from — let us say — Moravia, happens upon a deserted shore of the United States, plants firm the Moravian flag and declares this country to be the exclusive property of the Moravian king. An absurd proposition to say the least. Yet how closely it resembles in some respects the landing of Christopher Columbus on soil that had for millennia been inhabited by Native Americans. Is it not ironic that some five centuries later, we still honor Columbus as the "discoverer" of America — when, in fact, he did no such thing?

We believe that our actions initiate results, that inventors invent, that composers compose, that discoverers discover. According to kabbalistic philosophy, this is a fallacy. Kabbalah teaches that the most anyone can hope to do is to reveal what already is. As the old saying tells us, there is nothing new under the sun. Everything that ever was or will be must of necessity have been present in the En Sof before the Thought of Creation. The seeds of all ideas and inventions great and small are therefore around us and within us, awaiting revealment. Thus, by aligning our thoughts and actions with the needs of our time we can make ourselves worthy of being channels through which some truth or great discovery might be expressed.

### Growth

What causes growth? Why do seeds become trees? Why is the physical universe expanding? In a word the answer is desire. Desire draws energy to itself. The only time there is a lessening of expansion is when there is a lessening of desire.

There is no physical connection between the seed and the root of a tree, the root and the branch, the trunk and the leaf. Yet obviously there must be a relationship of some kind between these various elements, a bond which must somehow be enclosed within the makeup of the seed. The seed is the blueprint for the tree. The tree exists within the seed. The entire growth cycle of the tree, from birth through death, is included in the seed. The same may be said of the En Sof which is the seed of physical creation.

Just as the seed cannot jump to a branch, nor can the First Three of the Line, (Keter, Hokhmah, Binah) of the phase of Hokhmah, reveal the ten sefirot of Hokhmah of the circular vessels because the injection of empty space of the seven lower sefirot have become part of the growth. The seven of Keter precedes the First Three of Line of Hokhmah. Consequently these seven fill the gap between Keter of the circular vessels and Hokhmah of the circular vessels. The fourth level of each phase (Malkhut) provides the impetus for the evolution of each subsequent phase.

Growth is something we share with all things physical. Spiritual and intellectual, growth is our only method of relieving the burden of Bread of Shame. Thus, the kabbalist strives to close the gap between him or herself and the Light within. To not do so is to remain in the illusion of darkness.

Physical birth, growth and death, according to the kabbalistic wisdom, are of consequence only in the realm of the illusion. The death of the body's desire has no affect whatever on the soul, the striving and spiritual growth of which must continue through various lifetimes until the soul's corrective process (Tikune) is completed.

All that exists in the universe and all that ever will exist was included in the Endless before the Tsimtsum and will remain after all growth and expansion and Desire to Recive for oneself alone no longer serve a useful function. Thus, from the kabbalistic perspective, growth, like time, space, and matter is an illusion, though, of course, a necessary one.

Desire to Receive for oneself alone, itself is a product solely of the illusion, only of the Line. According to the kabbalistic tradition, that which is temporary, meaning all things physical, including striving (desire) and growth, are considered mere blips on the endless, timeless, unmoving grid of Infinity.

Thus growth is of vital importance to us. Indeed, if it were not for the striving that manifests as growth in this World of Action, we would have no way of completing our soul's Tikune, which is the very purpose of our physical existence. Indeed, all of the encircling Light that we can ever hope to reveal in this realm of illusion manifests as a result of the interaction between the Light and our receiving mechanism (Desire to Receive) which by its nature engenders growth.

### Zaddik

The term *zaddik*, meaning righteous, is reserved only for a blessed few. A zaddik is a holy man, a person of knowledge. Moses was a zaddik, as were all of the patriarchs. Shimon ben Yohai and Rabbi Isaac Luria also share that blessed name. A person who aspires to be a zaddik denies the world of illusion, rejects totally the Desire to Receive for Oneself Alone, and resists the yearnings of the body, favoring instead to follow only the mandates of the soul. Such persons are so completely devoid of the negative aspect of desire that when the body of a zaddik expires it is said to remain in a state of almost perfect constitution.

As with any physical object on earth, the human body is subject to gravity, which is the manifestation of Earth's primal motivating influence, Desire to Receive for Itself Alone. The soul, however, operates beyond gravity's jurisdiction and hence is free to travel in its quest to complete the cycle of its correction, or *tikune*. Thus, while the body's natural inclination, is to succumb to gravitation and remain inactive and rooted to one spot, the tendency of the soul is to travel in its quest for restoration with the infinite Light, the *Or En Sof*.

Above the atmosphere, beyond the realm of gravity, everything becomes weightless. In space, it is the natural inclination of any physical object, given even so much as a modicum of momentum, to continue to move until such time as it falls under the influence of another, larger planetary body. In fact, removed completely from any gravitational influence, the object in question would travel for lightyears without changing direction or speed. By transcending the Desire to Receive for Oneself Alone, the zaddik connects with an altered state of consciousness which is spiritually comparable to that weightless condition, in that his consciousness is no longer anchored by the negativity which is the motivating influence in the world of Restriction.

The zaddik, at every opportunity, resists comfort and complacency, for those are aspirations of the body caused by Desire to Receive for Oneself Alone. Because of this, people whose concerns are only physical, meaning that they are ensconced in Desire to Receive for Oneself Alone, may look at a zaddik and mistakenly believe that he is suffering, when nothing could be further from the truth. The zaddik, by denying the trappings of comfort, rises above the world of personalities, illusion, and outward appearances, and connects with a higher consciousness which is activated by the positive aspect of desire, namely, Desire to Receive for the Sake of Sharing.

The zaddik's voluntary resistance causes a cancellation of Desire to Receive for Oneself Alone, which, of course, is the root of all wrongdoing, and thus is he able to transcend the negative realm. By transforming Desire to Receive into Desire to Receive for the Sake of Sharing, he rises above what kabbalists for convenience call the negative "one percent" which represents the illusionary "reality" with which we are presented on a day-to-day basis, and unites with the "ninety-nine percent," which is the true, Infinite reality of the *Or En Sof*. When the negative one percent has been transformed by sharing, the zaddik is no longer effected by the negative acts of mankind.

The sefirotic triumvirate, *Keter*, *Hokhmah*, and *Binah*, the "First Three," which are synonymous with the soul, are governed by the laws of gravity only insofar as they are housed within the physical body. The soul operates beyond the laws of time, space, and motion. Only humanity's finite lower seven sefirot (the body) are subject to the laws that govern the physical world. Only the lower seven are constrained by gravity, air pressure, and the aging process. Removed from the confines of the body, our Infinite aspect is capable of infinite movement at infinite speed.

When negativity, the *klippot*, which manifests as a result of Desire to Receive for Oneself Alone, has been converted to the positive energy through an attitude of sharing, one no longer is affected by negativity. Thus transformed, the zaddik exists on a level of consciousness that is higher by far than that which is experienced by the so-called average person, though in all respects but one the former and the latter are the same — the only difference being that the so-called average person's consciousness is tuned-in to the lower frequency (the lower seven) while the zaddik's receiving mechanism is set on the higher frequency of the First Three. True, the body of a zaddik exists, like everyone else's, in the World of Restriction, but his consciousness remains above the petty machinations of negativity caused by material existence.

Only in the consciousness of this World of Restriction does chaos reign supreme. Above that lowest state of "body consciousness," there exists the infinite, endless, true reality of the *Or En Sof*, the reality with which the zaddik is continually connected. Thus, the zaddik's self denial should in no way be mistaken for suffering. The zaddik denies the body's desire for comfort and complacency in order to satisfy the much stronger and more important directives of the soul. Not unlike the negative pole of the filament of a light bulb, which denies electricity and thus produces light, by resisting the negative, represented by stasis and complacency, the zaddik reveals the positive, eternal, infinite Light of his own existence. For whereas the lower seven, being of a finite nature, can never achieve more than a transitory fulfillment; the connection made by the zaddik through positive resistance is with the eternal.

**Coming Full Circle**

From the Infinite perspective, we are, each of us,

permeated, filled to the capacity, with endless illumination. Spiritually, we lack for nothing. Lack is an illusion, though a necessary one, for it gives us our only opportunity of relieving Bread of Shame. This fact alone, however, does not oblige us to grope blindly in spiritual darkness. The purpose of the original restriction was to impart to man an element of free will sufficient for the removal of Bread of Shame. We have a choice in the matter of spirituality, the extent of which rests in our ability to recognize the negative Desire to Receive for the Self Alone and consciously act against it.

Spiritual circuitry requires conscious resistance. Either we restrict and reveal the Light or we do not restrict and remain in darkness. Unless by his voluntary resistance man acts contrary to the negative aspect of Desire, the purpose of his existence will never be revealed. This principle of kabbalistic metaphysics was established at the Tsimtsum and it will remain with us until Bread of Shame has been completely alleviated and the Tikune process, the cycle of spiritual correction, has come full circle. Only then will we as a species again receive the Light's blessing without the need for our conscious intervention in behalf of the Light.

Unlike the negative pole of the filament of a light bulb, man has the option of restricting in order to bring forth the unique Light of his existence. Thus, the kabbalist adopts an ongoing attitude of restriction, for by so doing, he or she dispels the illusion and brings Light to himself and the world. When one consciously resists the negative impulse of Desire to Receive for the Self Alone, a new and blissful state of consciousness is achieved in which the negative aspect of desire is converted into the positive Desire to Receive for the Sake of Sharing. This simple mechanism has the unique capability of erasing all illusions.

Just as the positive polarity seeks to fulfill the desire of the negative, the Emanator wants nothing more than to satisfy our every desire. In fact, kabbalists believe that every wish is immediately fulfilled on the level of the metaphysical and that all one must do to receive the benefit of that wish is to reject the impulse which first brought it into being. The paradox is that when man's negative polarity, which is expressed as the illusion of lack, accepts the Light which is freely offered, none of his spiritual potential is revealed, but if he rejects the Light then, contrarily, all of his potential is manifested.

The moment we experience the illusion of lack, the moment we feel deprived of love, of companionship, of money or creature comforts, and we are conscious of it, that is the moment to exercise voluntary restriction, for by so doing the illusion of lack is dispelled. Conscious resistance of this nature establishes a circuit with the Light which banishes the illusion of darkness to the nether-regions of one's existence.

Consciousness, from the kabbalistic viewpoint, consists of a concerted and continuous effort to restrict the negative Desire to Receive for the Self Alone so as to convert it into the positive Desire to Receive for the Sake of Sharing. This, and not some misplaced need for self-depravation, is the reason why kabbalists restrict the impulse to accept for selfish reasons the Emanator's endless blessings. By refusing to succumb to the Desire to Receive for the Self Alone the kabbalist creates the circuitry necessary for his own unique fulfillment.

**A World of Difference**

The original text in which the Ari's disciples first described the principles of what would later be known as Lurianic Kabbalah contains reference to the Light "moving down" through the four phases of Emanation. Today, the extension of the Upper Light through the phases of Emanation is similarly termed "descent," which refers to the process by which the Light becomes increasingly "denser," or we might say more obscured by the illusion, as it "extends" from the En Sof.

Also, that which is "above," meaning closer to the *Or En Sof*, was designated as being "purer" than that which is "below," or closer to the level of consciousness found in this fourth phase, Malkhut, the World of Action. Thus, we say that the Light "descends" through the four phases from "above to below," the "higher," or "purer" levels being closer to the source, *Or En Sof*. The "lower," or "denser," levels being closer to the Curtain of this fourth phase, is the "Middle Point" where all Light is revealed.

To put this into a more functional perspective, let us consider a situation in which information is passed from one person to another, who then passes it on again, and so on. Generally speaking, each person, consciously or otherwise, modifies the information, embellishes and diminishes it, until eventually the original ideas can hardly be recognized. The information becomes "clothed," we might say, or obscured as it "extends" from its original source and "passes through" the various "vessels," the people through whom it is passing.

Fortunately, not all of our words and ideas are destined to "descend" into obscurity by the process of passing them on.

Some might actually be improved and elevated, if those to whom we are speaking are motivated by Desire to Receive for the Sake of Sharing. In such instances, the illusionary process is superceded through the principle of Returning Light.

Take for example the so-called Think Tanks in which scholars meet to formulate new concepts, or the simple "brainstorming sessions" in which friends get together to create something for the common good. In situations such as these, the participants sometimes speak in terms of "bouncing ideas" off one another, a concept that demonstrates the kabbalistic principle of Returning Light.

When we are motivated by Desire to Receive for the Sake of Sharing we trigger the principle of Returning Light and instead of becoming more dense or clothed with illusion our ideas can become elevated by the process of reflective interaction. In our Think Tank example the motivating influence of the people involved is more likely to be Desire to Receive for the Sake of Sharing than the negative Desire to Receive for the Self Alone and thus the participants are apt to be rewarded with results that surpass their original intentions. Whereas when little or no resistance is established, such as in our first example, the original ideas are apt to be lost as they "descend" into what we might call an ever-deepening abyss of illusion.

In this world of illusion everything must go through process of "descent," meaning that it must traverse the gap between the positive polarity and the negative. The extent of our free will rests in our ability exercise the principle of Returning Light, such as in our example of the brainstorming session, and thus remove ourselves from the illusion by relieving Bread of Shame. Or we can exercise no resistance, such as in our first example, and remain in the world of illusion.

The Light's only aspiration is to fill us with its endless abundance, to restore to us a condition of complete spiritual and also of material contentment. However, the Light relinquished the ability to reveal its endless blessing at the time of the Tsimtsum. Had it not done so we would have no way of relieving Bread of Shame. And that is why it is up to us to reveal the infinite Light of our beings and to bring spiritual and material abundance to our lives. With an attitude of restriction, meaning resistance to Desire to Receive for the Self Alone, we can defeat the illusion and reveal the Light within.

# Part Four

# Art of Living

18

*The One Percent Solution*

ONLY A MINUTE FRACTION OF PHYSICAL REALITY, LET US for the sake of this discussion say one percent, is dominated by Desire to Receive for the Self Alone. The other ninety-nine percent, which represents that aspect of existence that we share with all things animal, vegetable, and mineral, is not influenced in the least by the negative aspect of desire. The one percent is the source of all of our problems. It is the one percent that harbors all of our illusions. And thus it is only that one percent which we must restrict in order to reveal the totality of our endless illumination.

According to the ancient kabbalistic wisdom, the animal, vegetal, and mineral kingdoms are essentially the same, the only difference being that the higher levels of the chain of life possess more Desire to Receive than the lower levels. Unlike the animal, vegetable, and mineral kingdoms, man alone has the ability, and it might be said the burden, of having to turn on the switch, so to speak, to reveal Light. All other beings and inanimate objects have an instinctual mechanism with which to reveal endless illumination.

All matter possesses Desire to Receive. Yet man and man alone is obliged to restrict the negative facet of desire in order to alleviate Bread of Shame. The difference between a man and an animal rests solely in man's ability and obligation to restrict the minuscule fragment of his existence (the one percent) which is dominated by the negative aspect of desire. Man can switch it on or off, meaning he can either restrict, thereby creating a circuit, or he can succumb to Desire to Receive for the Self Alone and remain in spiritual darkness. Only when we trigger the energy-intelligence of restriction does our Light become revealed.

### 99.44% Pure

A certain soap commercial attests to its product being 99.44% pure. And yet it is quite amazing how many people are allergic to that product and break out in hives every time they use it. Such is the nature of impurity. A speck of dirt can, for some people, make a bowl of soup unappetizing. A spoonful of PCB's can contaminate an entire reservoir, making millions of gallons of water undrinkable.

A little impurity goes a long way.

A similar situation exists in the world as it relates to the illusion. The illusion of darkness comprises only a tiny fraction of the entire cosmic picture, let us say one percent. The other ninety-nine percent is Light, the true Reality. However, the vast majority of people live in only the illusion. Where there is Light, they see darkness; where there is good, they see evil; where there is truth, they see only fiction.

Why, if there's so much reality around are we so blind to its presence?

The answer, of course, like the answer to every question, can be found in the En Sof before the Thought of Creation. Remember, it was we who asked to share in the process of creation and by so doing caused the reign of darkness to prevail. Thus we have no one to blame if we are slaves to the illusion and darkness rules our lives.

Evil is an illusion that is animated by our failure to act against it. Through resistance, we can liberate the Light and in the process free ourselves. When the one percent is dominated by the energy-intelligence of Desire to Receive for the Self Alone darkness seems to encompass everything, even the ninety-nine percent which is the Light. This, of course, is an illusion. No negative impulse can exist in the endless presence of the *Or En Sof*. By succumbing to the negative aspect of Desire we allow the darkness to triumph over the Light. Contrarily, by converting the negative aspect of desire (Desire for the Self Alone) into the positive (Desire for the Sake of Sharing) we end the reign of darkness and the Light is again revealed.

In the Messianic Age much will change as a result of a simple conversion of energy. Desire to Receive for the Self

Alone will be converted into Desire to Receive for the Sake of Sharing. Thus the fraction of Reality that is now obscured by illusion will disappear. For some that age is here today. For those who understand and exercise the principle of resistance in their daily lives, the illusion of darkness holds little sway. The object, then, for the kabbalist, is to achieve an altered state of consciousness by which he or she can remove the illusion and again unveil the Light.

### The Shortest Distance Between Two Points

According to the laws of geometry, the shortest distance between two points is a straight line. This is true in the world of illusion. In Reality, however, meaning from the Infinite perspective, the shortest distance between any two points is a circle. By creating a circuit of energy, meaning a circular connection with the Light, one is instantly connected with everything, everywhere, which, according to Kabbalah, is not only the shortest distance between two points, but the only connection truly worth making.

### Success and Failure

Desire to Receive is comprised of two aspects, Desire to Receive for Oneself Alone and Desire to Receive for the Sake of Sharing. The former is a bi-product of the Line, the latter emerges from the Circle. Kabbalah therefore designates the former as illusionary while the latter is deemed real. Of all the life forms and energy-intelligences in the animal, vegetable, and mineral kingdoms, we (Mankind) alone are subject to the snares and entanglements created by false desires stemming from the impure, linear illusion, for only we have been given the opportunity and the responsibility of alleviating Bread of Shame.

No thought, deed, or endeavor will ever succeed on anything other than the illusionary level if it is based in the impure aspect of Desire to Receive. Those ventures that are motivated by false desires lead inevitably to failure. Therefore, one may look at almost any failure, defeat, or lack of attainment and instantly conclude that it was borne of an impure (false) cause.

Yet personal failures should not necessarily be looked upon with regret. They can be viewed as lessons, opportunities for correction, re-connecting mechanisms in the circle of spiritual adjustment, transformation and reincarnation. Kabbalistically speaking there is only one true criterion for the measurement of success or failure and that is how well one succeeds in determining and applying the singular activity by which each of us recreates affinity with the Light.

How is it that some people seem impervious to their failures while others are totally debilitated by them?

Those who measure themselves according to standards prescribed by others, by the media, by the educational system, by conventional societal dictates or the narrow precepts imposed by dogmatic religious beliefs are far more apt to suffer as a result of failure than are those who measure success and failure according to their own unique requirements. Inevitably those who succeed must meet certain personal prerequisites, but certainly these have little or nothing to do with the conventional injunctions foisted upon us by the illusionary material dream. It means nothing to succeed according to the standards of others if one does not also succeed according to his or her own ethics and principles.

The moment we acknowledge a failure as something other than a lesson and an opportunity for correction we give it credence and establish it as a reality. And so we find that measuring ourselves against the standards set by others makes us immediately susceptible to this debilitating syndrome. Kabbalah teaches that one should never see oneself as lacking in anything, for the very acknowledgement of deficiency creates deficiency, as does the acceptance of failure establish failure. Is it not more prudent and desirable to avoid as much as possible the debilitating carousel of self depravation that revolves around false comparisons?

The only reality in this world is the eternal aspect that results from restriction. Thus the kabbalist restricts lack and resists deficiency, for by so doing he or she creates affinity with the first act of restriction, Tsimtsum. The *Or En Sof* is immeasurable in its perfection. We too have an element of perfection, an Infinite aspect that transcends finite comparisons and limited rational understanding. Only the finite, limited, corporeal aspect of ourselves is imperfect, and that facet of our existence, as has been well established, is illusion. Therefore the only success that can be gained by gratifying false linear (finite) desires is false success which by any real standard can only be deemed failure.

**Permanent and Temporary Remnant**

The Ari, Rabbi Isaac Luria stated that, "... in the matter of the devolvement of the Light from place to place, there are two forms of remnant in the places traversed: the first is 'permanent remnant,' which means the mixing and binding with the Light already found at the level, the two lights becoming one as if they had always been one; the second is merely 'temporary remnant,' in other words there is no mixing and binding with the Light found there. The Lights remain distinct." He further stated that, "... the Light of the line, which traverses the levels of Circles, does not do so as permanent remnant but merely as temporary remnant, to teach us that it is not mixed with the Light of the Circles to form one phase, rather it is found there distinct and in its own phase."

This abstruse-sounding text, when deciphered, reveals a number of kabbalistic truths and has various practical applications. First, though, let us attempt to explain or otherwise allay such questions as might be raised by the language of what has been stated thus far. What did the Ari mean by words such as "traverses," "passes," and "devolvement"? Was he not speaking of Light which kabbalists believe to be endless, timeless and perfectly still? If, as the kabbalists say, the Light is everywhere, how can it possibly traverse anything? And if It is eternal and Infinitely abundant, how can It accurately be spoken of in terms of "devolvement," and "moving from place to place"?

Again we confront the difficulty in attempting to describe deeply spiritual images with common language. Only from the illusionary, "finite" perspective does movement of any kind seem to occur. From the Light's perspective, nothing moves from place to place, or devolves, or diminishes through the successive stages of emanation. Light is everywhere, at the center of the earth, at the bottom of the sea, in darkest space, in the marrow of our bones. So in Reality, meaning from the Infinite perspective, nothing whatever happens to the Light; Its energy is ubiquitous and never-changing.

What the Ari was attempting to impart is that the circular vessels, which might aptly be described as "the real me," encompass everything that one will ever acquire in the way of knowledge, but because of the Tikune process and our need to absolve Bread of Shame, the circular vessels, of necessity, although they are here, ever-present, and although they completely permeate every level of earthly and metaphysical existence, must, because of the illusionary process, appear from our limited, "finite" perspective in the illusionary world as if they do not exist.

By "passing" the Ari was referring to information of any kind that fails to make an impression upon us. Obviously some information makes a distinct impression upon us while other information "passes" as we say "over our heads." Some knowledge is "etched" into our memory banks, while other knowledge "goes in one ear and out the other." That information which seems to "pass through" is termed "temporary remnant," while that which remains, becoming a permanent part of our finite consciousness, was termed by the Ari to be "permanent remnant."

The circular Lights, our inner encircling vessels, contain all of the information, all of the knowledge and the wisdom, that one can ever hope to possess. In terms of the Infinite picture, the Light of the Circles certainly preceded the light of the Line (everything originated from the Circular Light), however, from our limited perspective the opposite is true: it is the light of the Line which precedes the light of the Circles, for only when the latter connects with the former is any Infinite illumination revealed to us. The Light of Circles is always here. It is simply concealed from our view until it is acted upon by the Light of the Line.

As to the matter of permanent and temporary remnant, we all realize that certain information remains with us while other information seems never to become embedded in our consciousness and subsequently seems to disappear. Does this have anything to do with the information or the medium through which the information was coming to us? For instance, if a good teacher makes an important point while we happen to be daydreaming, is this any fault of the teacher? Of course not. Is the information the teacher was trying to impart in any way lessened by our failure to listen? Yes, but only from our point of view. For another example, let us examine a situation in which the sun is shining but we choose to remain in the shade of an umbrella. Is the sun in any way affected by our decision to remain hidden from it? No, only from our perspective beneath the umbrella does the light of the sun seem to be diminished. It was this same phenomenon that the Ari was referring to when he made the distinction between permanent and temporary remnant.

An old kabbalistic saying serves as an apt illustration of permanent and temporary remnant. "Some people live seventy years as one day, others live one day as seventy years." Except in the case of *zaddikim* such as Moses or the Ari, who are totally connected to the Light and thus require no spiritual correction, a life without change is not a life worth living. If no change takes place in a person's life, meaning that if a person goes through life without making any attempt to connect with the reality, the Circular Light of his or her inner being, there can be no spiritual correction, which after all is the purpose of our earthly existence.

It is up to us to consciously form connections with and thus reveal the permanent remnant within us. To not do so is to derive no more from our lives than if we had lived only one day. Light is revealed through the illusionary process, for that is the world we exist in. We must make every attempt to capture the Light of the "real me," otherwise life passes by and we reveal nothing of our Infinite nature.

This is what the Ari was referring to when he stated that, "The Light of the Line which traverses the levels of Circles does not do so as "permanent remnant," but merely as "temporary remnant." The circles are within us, and they contain everything that the line will ever provide them with, but unfortunately we need the illusionary process because that is our only way of removing Bread of Shame. It is for this reason that kabbalists consider the light of the line to be of far greater importance than the light of the Circles.

So it must be until that day when the cycle of our spiritual correction is complete and we return to our place of ultimate spiritual fulfillment within the endless Circle of the *Or En Sof*.

**All Vibration is Music**

Like life itself, sound contains many levels and frequencies, some which are beyond the range of our perceptions, others which are not. Each of us listens at different emotional, intellectual, and spiritual frequencies, depending on various factors and variables. Our mood can play a part in what we hear, our attitude, our frame of mind, what kind of day we've had, what kind of pressures we are experiencing in our lives.

A hundred people may attend a lecture and each will come away with a different perspective on what the lecturer was attempting to say. Some will feel uplifted by the presentation, others may feel defeated. Also it is quite possible for a speaker to be sending messages which he or she had no intention of sending but which can still be readily comprehended by someone who is listening on a different frequency.

What we hear, then, depends largely on how we listen, and what we are able to perceive has less to do with the words that are spoken than on the direction and focus of the listener's ear. For example, some people have the unfortunate tendency of attempting to manipulate everything they hear so as to make it fit a certain ideology or obsession which for selfish reasons they happen to be attached or to which they are habitually tied. These people are not really listening and hence they do not really hear.

Sound, all sound, because it is ephemeral, is considered from the kabbalistic perspective to be illusionary. However, as with all that is of this World of Action, sound too embodies a large measure of Infinity. Thus if one listens intently, and if one's desire to receive is properly aligned and focused, and if one makes no attempt to manipulate the sounds that he or she is hearing so as to fit a selfish preconception, there is no reason why one might not find infinite delight in virtually any sound, from the babbling of a brook, to the ranting of an idiot, or even in the barking of a dog.

This is why it is possible for a wise man to listen to the words of a fool and hear wisdom, while another who may possess a genius I.Q., but who is motivated by Desire to Receive for the Self Alone, may sit for years at the feet of an intellectual or spiritual master and not understand a single word. For the kabbalist every sound holds the potential for union with the highest states of his or her spiritual existence.

## Creative Disengagement

So conditioned have we become to living under the iron hand of the material illusion that today we serve the illusion which poses as reality and to pay tribute to its dominance, praying before the alter of the modern deities, Science and Technology, genuflecting as the seemingly endless parade of material "progress" marches by. The great kabbalistic paradox, and one of the more lamentable ironies of this modern age, is that the so-called "reality" that we allow to rule us with impunity is a total illusion, whereas the so-called "fantasy world" (thoughts, dreams, daydreams, imaginings, meditation), so soundly maligned by many self-proclaimed "realists," is much closer to being real.

According to the ancient wisdom of Kabbalah, reality diminishes in direct proportion to physicality. Thus, resistance to the finite material illusion is the key to unlocking the door to gates of the only true reality, that of the Infinite. By challenging the material illusion, one creates a circuit with the alternate universe of the mind and becomes a channel for higher states of consciousness. This is true control; this, not the tyranny of the material illusion, is the root of real self-determination and the way by which to transform life's negative polarity into the positive.

That which you resist you draw to you, that which you resist you become.

**On Death and Dying**

Did Moses die? The Torah says yes; the Kabbalah, however, says no. How can this seeming discrepancy be reconciled? The answer is that both opinions are correct, depending on one's point of view. From the finite perspective (meaning the limited vista seen from the illusionary world), yes, it is true that Moses died. From the Infinite perspective, however, he is still alive. The death spoken of in the Torah is the death of the illusion, the Desire to Receive for the Self Alone.

Friction, gravity, and air pressure will eventually cause a top to stop spinning. Consider, though, the possibility that the thought that sets a top in motion might continue on even after the body of the top has ceased turning, even for all time. In a frictionless environment a top would presumably spin forever. The spiritual realm is impervious to friction. Being without material substance, the Light of our beings is the state of the art in perpetual motion. Like a top set spinning in space, it is not subject to physical tribulations.

That part of us which is of the Light is not prone to change or decomposition. Only the body, the intelligence of which is desire to receive, is susceptible to aging and death. The body dies, but the Infinite aspect of a person lives on in circles of return.

To die, then, is merely to shed that which is influenced by gravity and friction, namely, Desire to Receive for the Self Alone. Disease can kill a body, not a soul. Accidents, pain and suffering, catastrophes, chaos and confusion are all of the physical world. The world of the spirit, though it is in the same place as this world, functions in a state of utter stillness and tranquility, far beyond the stifling influence of gravity and other physical limitations.

That is not to say that the physical aspect of humanity is not also of the Endless. All that was of the Endless still is of the Endless. Every speck of matter is endowed with the Infinite Presence and also with Desire to Receive for Itself Alone. Every thing in this world has its roots in Endlessness, and to the Infinite it will always belong.

Certainly it is true that the physical body decomposes upon death, but the material constituents of the body do not expire or disappear. The material merges with other components to form new objects and organisms. Nothing happens to the material itself. Change occurs only within the shaping influence that keeps each object or organism in its present form, namely, each individual organism's Desire to Receive for the Self Alone.

Physical death, then, is the dissolution of the body's Desire to Receive — this and nothing more. Only that which is negative, meaning controlled by Desire to Receive, is subject to change. However, although it is negative, Desire to Receive for the Self alone, also affords us our only opportunity to relieve Bread of Shame. Until one sheds all Desire to Receive for the Self Alone, he or she is obliged to return to this world of illusion to continue the process of correction.

Did Moses die? Yes and no. His body ceased to function as a vessel for Desire to Receive, but his spiritual legacy, his energy, that which transcended Desire to Receive for the Self Alone, lives on. To the extent that Moses was physical, to the extent that physicality includes Desire to Receive for the Self Alone, Moses died, but that part of him that transcended Desire to Receive lives even today.

Rabbi Ashlag, in his translation of the Zohar, spoke eloquently of the death of Moses when he wrote that, "By his death he added more light, more life to the world."

**Two Points of View**

Let us, for the sake of argument, pit the pessimist's view of life against that of the optimist.

The pessimist tells us that war and deception, death and duplicity, nationalism, ethnocentrism, terrorism — the trademarks of this modern age — are manifestations of the true nature of humanity. Man, he tells us, is an irredeemable villain, an incorrigible criminal, a rapist, a killer, a liar, and a cheat. He asserts that the world is populated by a virtual gang of thugs called the human race, most of whom would just as soon stab you in the back as give you a second glance, and concludes his argument with a statement to the effect that the living hell of violence, torture, starvation and terminal disease that man is harvesting is the price he must pay for the seeds of evil he has sown — a retribution for which he is only too well deserving.

Next the optimist stands before us holding up a sprig of leaves. He challenges us to look closely at the miracle which is a leaf and then try to tell him that this world is not a wondrous place. Life, he tells us, is two lovers on a sun-drenched meadow, it is a drop of dew on a cactus in the first light of a desert morning, it is a river that runs to the ocean, it is the miracle of procreation. Love, he asserts, is the motivating force in the world. Yes, bad things happen, unfortunate, isolated incidents, but the bad is far outweighed by the good. People, at the core, the optimist assures us, are good and honest. In conclusion he states that we should be grateful for this life — for each day is a joy and a blessing, and each and every one of us is a jewel of creation.

Which one are we to believe?

Of course, by now the student of Kabbalah is aware that the chasm between ourselves and the Light of Creation was of our own making — for by demanding individuation from the Creator we also inherited the responsibility of re-illuminating our Encircling Vessels and thus absolving Bread of Shame. The separation between ourselves and what kabbalists call the real world — meaning the world of the Endless — causes us to be oblivious to the Infinite Light around us. The world we do see, the negative world of Illusion and Restriction, while it represents only the smallest fraction of the big picture, the grand scheme of things, it is still the world that most of us deal with exclusively.

So who is right, the pessimist or the optimist? Is this world a living heaven or a living hell? It all depends on one's point of view. From the perspective of the lower seven we see the negative side of existence, from the point of view of the upper three we see the positive. The kabbalist seeks to bridge the gap between the two through the art of well-tempered resistance.

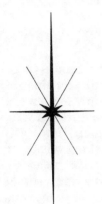

## The Candlemaker

LONG AGO AND FAR AWAY THERE LIVED A POOR candlemaker whose name has been forgotten, but whom, for the purpose of our story, we will call, Sefi. Perhaps not the brightest of men — no, he was *definitely* not the brightest — still, our poor Sefi would have to be ranked among the most virile men of his or any other age — and that is no exaggeration. In fact, if the truth be known, we can assume with more than a small likelihood of accuracy that at least a few of the townsfolk must have whispered accusations declaring Sefi to be some kind of crazed sex fiend. Indeed, he had sired some seventy-eight children which now, alas, he found that he could not support.

Twenty-seven years he had struggled in the candle trade
as had his father and his father before him, but at a time in
life when men who had chosen other occupations were
retiring or dying peacefully in their beds of natural causes,
Sefi could entertain no such possibility. A man, after all,
cannot retire on nothing, and poor Sefi had nothing whatever
to show for his life, aside from a tired, sickly wife, a shoddy
little shop, and seventy-eight, or perhaps it was seventy-nine,
noisy, tattered children. As for dying in peace, that too was
unthinkable. In those days there was no such thing as life
insurance, and had there been he would not have been able to
afford to keep up the payments on the premiums — and so it
was that our Sefi could not even die in good conscience for it
would mean leaving his family with nothing, which in those
days of severe taxation and monetary deflation was actually
worth some three and one half percent less than nothing.

Oh, what a shambles his life had become!

Day after troubled day he racked his brain in search of a
solution. Night after sleepless night he paced a serpentine
path between the bodies of his children who slept scattered
about on the floor of their tiny kitchen. To say that our Sefi
had reached the bottom of his emotional barrel might well be
understating the point. His credit was extended to the limit,
there was barely enough food on the table, his wife would not
come near him, and twenty-three of his children needed
braces. He was, as they say, in the depths of despair, at the
end of his rope, and only a ghost of his former self. In fact,
in one telling of this story it is said that so low and
downtrodden had our poor hero become that he would have
committed suicide, but even for that he was too depressed.

An old woman hobbled into his shop one morning for the

purpose of purchasing a three cent candle. Sefi could not hide his sadness. The strain of his wretched life was etched into his every feature. Seeing the pale, dour figure of Sefi, and being of a kindly disposition, the old woman could not help feeling empathy for the shell of a man who stood before her with stooped shoulders and sad, sad eyes.

"Surely, young man, things cannot be as bad as all that," said the old woman, half between a statement and a question.

A rare smile came from nowhere to brighten Sefi's pallid countenance. "Young I am not, madame," answered Sefi, his smile fading, "but yes I'm afraid things are that bad, perhaps even worse."

And so it was that sensing his visitor had an ear well-tuned for listening, he poured out the details of his tale of woe. The old woman listened attentively and when Sefi's sad story ended there was a tear in the corner of one of her craggy eyes. "What a mess," she said at last. She rustled through her handbag for what Sefi thought perhaps might be a tissue, but instead the old woman came up with a small diamond and extended it toward him. "Take it."

Sefi resisted, weakly, but she pressed it on him.

"Take it, take it, young man, there are plenty more where it came from." Sefi took the diamond and whispered humble thanks. "And now," said the old woman, "it is my turn to talk."

She told him of a far off place called the Island of Diamonds where diamonds were as common as dirt is in most other parts of the world. Indeed, the old woman informed him that on this far away island of diamonds aplenty, a six month voyage by sea, the streets were paved with diamonds, and instead of bricks and mortar the houses were literally constructed of large diamonds and held together with glue made from seaweed and diamond dust. And she wrote on a scrap of paper the name and address of a seagoing captain who could make all of the arrangements.

"Thank you," said Sefi, again and again, and he filled her bags with as many candles as the old woman could possibly carry.

Our hero wasted no time. By the very next morning he had packed his bags and used the diamond given to him by the old woman to book passage for the Island of Diamonds. In his excitement to get to the island our Sefi lost track of the fact that his absence would deprive his wife and children of a provider for a period of almost two years, for it was a six month voyage to get to the island after which the ship would not return for another six at least, and finally there was a six month journey home.

Please, good reader, do not be misled concerning the nature of Sefi's true intentions. It was not greed that propelled him to make this long and arduous journey. He loved his family dearly and did briefly consider the hardship his long absence would cause, but this was truly the only way that he could think of to extricate himself and them from their intolerable impoverishment. And so it was with a sad heart that he set sail while his wife and children lined the dock, waving and crying miserably.

Of the actual journey all records have been lost to antiquity, and so we pick up our story six months later when the ship finally docks at the Island of Diamonds. How ecstatic our hero must have been when he disembarked after his long and arduous voyage to discover that everything was exactly as the old woman had described. Indeed, just as she had said, the streets were paved with them! Nearby mountains gleamed profusely with the sparkling light that was reflected by them. Diamonds were everywhere!

An hour had not passed before Sefi's sacks, which he had brought for the purpose, were brimming over with diamonds. Hardly could he walk the burden of his new found riches was so great. Only then did it occur to him that the ship would not be back for six months and it was obvious that the diamonds were not going anywhere. What sense was there in lugging around hundreds of pounds of diamonds in the meantime? And so, leaving his sacks of diamonds under a tree — secure in the knowledge that no one would steal them — our Sefi set about with only a few of the choicest ones which he would use to find food and accommodations.

Here, the story of Sefi takes a slight turn for the worse. It did not take our hero long to discover that diamonds, in addition to being as common as dirt on this Island of Diamonds, were equally as valuable. His diamonds, worth a king's ransom back home, were without even the slightest value. Despondency settled once again over our poor Sefi. Here he was in a worse situation than the one he left, for at least there he had a little food, and company (plenty of that!), and a roof over his head. It should not be said, though, that the people on the Island of Diamonds were completely heartless. One kindly shopkeeper did take pity on Sefi and gave him a bun in exchange for a perfect ten carat diamond, but only because he took a liking to its shape and thought it would be a nice decoration at the bottom of a goldfish bowl.

Night fell and Sefi nestled under the tree among his sacks of diamonds. Only then did it strike him that in the town there was not a light to be seen. None of the diamond houses had lights in the windows — the only light in the town, it seemed, was reflected light that echoed off the diamonds in the moonlight. Could it be that the people on the Island of Diamonds possessed no knowledge of candlemaking? He jumped up and ran through the streets looking for a lighted candle, but much to his delight he found not a single one.

And so it was that Sefi went into business making and selling candles. Within a week he had rented a small shop and already he had hundreds of customers queuing up to buy candles for whatever amount of the local currency Sefi saw fit to charge. To say he made a handsome living would be understating the case considerably — in fact he was successful beyond even his wildest dreams.

By the end of his stay our Sefi had parlayed his candlemaking skills into a string of shops and had become perhaps the richest and definitely the most popular man on the entire island. So grateful were the local townsfolk for the light that Sefi had shed on them that when the ship docked in preparation for the return journey, they assisted Sefi in loading it up with the product which had made him a wealthy man.

That night, as the ship set sail, Sefi could not contain his emotions. Tears streamed down his face — for all of the townsfolk had come to see him off, to wave and give their blessings. Candlelight created a beautiful nimbus above the town, for each of the island's inhabitants had lighted a candle in his honor. And so it was that the ship heaped high with candles steered away from the dock — but the sacks of diamonds remained under the same tree where Sefi had left them, forgotten.

We shall spare you, dear reader, the sordid details of Sefi's sad return to his former village, except to say that things got worse and they never got better.

Not surprisingly this story has a moral — for stories of this kind always do: Always remember from whence you came and to whence you must return.

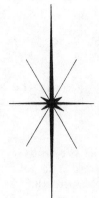

# 20

## *Crime and Punishment*

A**NSWER TRUE OR FALSE:**

A. Crime pays.

B. Most crimes go unpunished.

C. The more selfish one is, the more cutthroat, the higher one will be able to climb up the ladder of success.

D. Some people get away with murder.

E.   It is sometimes possible to cheat the system of restriction and receive for the self alone.

If you answered false to all of the above questions you are well on the way to becoming a kabbalist. No crime goes unpunished, no sin escapes retribution.

Ridiculous, you say? Outrageous! What about the thieves who are never caught? Look at all the loansharks and black-marketeers who amass fortunes through their shady dealings. Look at the risk arbitragers who make hundreds of millions trading on insider information. And what about the cocaine barons who have all but wrested control of certain South American governments?

True, in light of the evidence it would seem that no sane person could possibly deny that many people get away with all sorts of crimes, even murder, every day of the week. Many people profit from crime, but only from the perspective of the illusion.  In reality, meaning from the infinite perspective, the builder who cuts costs on hidden corners, the businessman who skims profits, the broker who trades on inside information, the thief, the killer, or anyone who benefits at the detriment of others, may achieve windfall profits and certainly has the ability to amass a mountain of material possessions, but if his or her actions were motivated solely by Desire to Receive for the Self Alone he or she will receive only the outward appearance of those acquisitions, the title to the goods, but not the goods  themselves, the things, but not their intrinsic value.

The material trappings accumulated by the person who is motivated by Desire to Receive for the Self Alone will be just that — traps — prisons from which the only escape is restriction. Instead of enjoyment, they will give him only grief. He may own many homes, but he will never feel at home in them. He may possess beautiful and priceless art objects, but they will impart less true pleasure to him than if they were dollar signs scrawled on a wall. As much time and effort as he might have expended, as difficult as his task might have been, as materially prosperous, as brilliant and incisive as his actions may have appeared to others, the person who is inspired by the negative aspect of desire will receive no lasting satisfaction from the spoils of his greed-motivated labors.

Ironically, all of the acquisitions accumulated by greedy people only cause them greater discomfort. If the same people were to restrict and thus remove the illusion, they would acquire the contentment that eludes them. That is the paradox of Returning Light: By saying yes to the impulse to receive for the self alone we get nothing, whereas by saying no to that same impulse we can, quite literally, "have it all."

When one negates the body's desire for comfort (especially in the form of luxury and opulence), one gives comfort to the soul. By choosing to remain in a state of unfulfillment the kabbalist acts as a filament, a third-column mediator, and thus is able to establish a circuit with the Light.

No doubt this concept would be scorned as something akin to blasphemy by the growing segment of the population that deifies money and worships at the feet of the rich and famous and has made a religion of material acquisition. Today the prevailing attitude seems to be that any means is justified if it comes to a profitable end. And, indeed, statistics seem to bear out the fact that the majority of crimes do go unpunished. And certainly we can all cite examples of criminals and businessmen who have made millions by taking advantage of those less fortunate than themselves. Nonetheless, it is a fallacy to think that money and material possessions will automatically bring us fulfillment. The only act that imparts true contentment is restriction.

The illusion is given weight and substance by our thoughts and actions. By accepting the illusion as our reality we make it real. The thief sustains the illusion, as does the cocaine baron, the inside trader, and all people who better themselves at the expense of others. The person who succumbs to the negative aspect of desire perpetuates the illusion, whereas the kabbalist, by his or her resistance, destroys the illusion and reveals the Light. The difference between the kabbalist and the person who is motivated by the negative aspect of desire is that whereas the latter, the thief, the inside trader, the greed-motivated businessman, attempts to achieve fulfillment by satisfying the Desire to Receive for the Self Alone, the kabbalist achieves true fulfillment by rejecting that same impulse.

Failure to restrict the negative aspect of desire produces a short circuit which causes one to remain in a state of robotic consciousness. Surrendering to the illusion perpetuates the darkness and imparts pleasure to no one. The conscience of the person who is motivated by the negative aspect of desire carries a heavy burden, the weight of illusion, the darkness, the blindness that is the constant companion of Desire to Receive for the Self Alone. The kabbalist, contrarily, has no excess freight to carry; his conscience is clean, his vision unobstructed.

Fulfillment exists only in the real world, the endless

world in which the Desire to Receive for the Self Alone has absolutely no influence. Desire to Receive for the Self Alone preserves the illusion; voluntary resistance destroys it. Restriction creates an altered state of consciousness by which to bridge the gap between ourselves and the Light.

The Creator restricted His benevolence so that we the emanated would have a way of absolving Bread of Shame. Through conscious, voluntary resistance we impart pleasure to the Creator and also bring Light into our lives. By paying tribute to the original act of restriction, the Tsimtsum, which we do when we resist and thus expose the illusion we enable the Light to be revealed. For illusion cowers in the presence of Reality; darkness cannot exist where there is Light.

The goal of the kabbalist, then, is to redirect his or her thought processes in such a way as to bring about the end of the reign of the illusion and restore illumination to the world and also, as a consequence, to him or herself. This may strike the reader as being at best a difficult, if not an impossible, task until one considers that despite its seeming omniscience, the one percent that is illusion has a very tenuous existence that even a small degree of resistance can easily destroy. Even a little resistance can illuminate a large, dark space. Light a match in a totally darkened airplane hangar and every corner will, at least to some small degree, be exposed.

Such is the beauty of Returning Light.

Thus, through conscious resistance, does the kabbalist serve the needs of both Light and vessel. By transforming the negative aspect of desire into the positive he or she exposes the illusion of darkness to the Light of reality. Light is everywhere, ready, willing, and able, at the slightest provocation (resistance), to reveal its endless presence. Through conscious resistance to the Desire to Receive for the Self Alone the kabbalist acts in the manner of a match in an airplane hangar, or the filament in a light bulb, establishing a circuitous flow of energy, which in turn creates, even from a small amount of resistance, a wide circle of Light.

This considered, let us return to the question: does crime pay? No, those who engage in crime merely serve to perpetuate the illusion. The same is true of all those who succumb to the Desire to Receive for the Self Alone. While it may seem as though the criminal is escaping punishment for his crimes, and the "shrewd" captains of commerce and industry, who seemingly let nothing or no one stand in their way, are prospering at the expense of others, in reality, the thief is stealing from himself, the killer is committing suicide, the inside trader is trading in his soul. In the real world no crime goes unpunished, no sin escapes retribution.

## A Fable of Two Brothers

Long ago, in a village far away, there lived two brothers who were as different as two people could possibly be. In fact, you could search the whole world over and be unlikely to discover two young men with so little in common. For whereas the elder was studious, the younger cared nothing for books and learning; and while the elder was courteous, the younger tended to be quite rude; and though the elder ate and drank moderately, the younger ate gluttonously and drank like a proverbial fish.

The elder brother, you see, aspired to be a *zaddik*, a

righteous one, and to that end he applied himself with unmitigated diligence. Early in life, he had been called by some deep, inner longing to live an austere and ascetic existence. And so, in deference to those whom he considered his spiritual forbears, the righteous ones of old, he prayed and studied the ancient wisdom, resisted comfort and complacency, and avoided, as much as was humanly possible, all earthly pleasures — all, that is, save one. The sole diversion he did allow himself, if it could be called that, was to sing, each evening, a single hymn of jubilation.

The positive example set by the elder brother was, needless to say, not for a moment emulated by the younger. Quite to the contrary, the only mandates which the younger brother was interested in fulfilling were those of his untamed libido. Indeed, it was with deliberation equal to that of his older brother's piety and goodness, that the younger engaged in all manner of hedonistic and reckless pursuits. His profligacy had made him a local legend, and, verily, the infamy was well deserved. *Eat, drink and be merry!* might well have been his motto, although, *Live for today for tomorrow we may die!* would have just as aptly applied. For he could eat any three men under the table, and was sometimes heard to threaten that he might one day drink the entire county dry — a threat which was not lightly taken. The life of any party, and quite a lady's man, too, the younger brother was always accompanied by a coterie of loose woman (though they did cling tightly to him!) and a cluster of friends and hangers-on.

For fear that the reader might credit the younger brother's popularity to wit, charisma, charm, or even to his vainly handsome appearance, it should be explained that such was anything but the case. Nor should the younger's renowned generosity be mistaken as an emblem of a compassionate heart. No, alas, neither was the circumstance. In truth, the state of affairs that existed then was no different from the one that endures to this day, meaning that it has never been terribly difficult to find those who will gladly assist one in squandering an inheritance, no matter how meager it may happen to be. And as for the younger's generosity, it was born not from kindness, but rather from guilt, so deeply ingrained that it was not even perceived by him, much less admitted to. For, unlike the elder brother who had been a good and dutiful son, the younger had rarely lifted so much as a finger in his late father's behalf.

Additionally, lest the reader be inundated by mistaken impressions, it must also be clarified, before this humble parable advances one sentence further, that the notable contrast in their personalities caused the brothers to harbor no great animosity toward each other. Despite their differences, there was, in fact, hardly a morsel of enmity between them. Their upbringing by a kindly merchant, recently deceased, and a loving, doting mother, instilled in them tolerance and a disposition to live and let live, and, accordingly, they got on well for the most part — though, to be sure, neither approved of the other's *modus operandi* and they did have their share of arguments, as brothers tend to do. Always, though, in the end, when the heat of the battle cooled, all would be forgiven.

So it came as no great surprise when the two brothers bid farewell to their separate circles of friends, and gave their mother farewell kisses and numerous assurances of their safe return, and set out walking one sunny morning in the late spring of the year 1653 toward a distant mecca of art, commerce and culture. Nor should it strain any reasonable reader's credulity to discover that their intended aims and expectations for making this journey, like the brothers themselves, were as different as darkness and light. For whereas the elder brother hoped to find a certain zaddik who was rumored to be seeking a spiritual apprentice, and whom he would humbly beg to aid him in his quest to himself become a righteous one, the younger brother, contrarily, had heard tales of the city's many lewd and lascivious pleasures, of which he hoped to sample all but a few.

The days passed amicably. Mile after mile, village after village, county after county, they walked, conversing and arguing good-naturedly, occasionally pausing to gaze upon some uncommon sight, to hear some unusual sound, or to rest and eat by the banks of an algae-laden pond or a fast-running brook. By night, though, they went their separate ways. While the elder brother read the Torah by firelight, meditated, and sang his nightly hymn, the younger brother, depending on their proximity to a town or village, would either eat and drink himself into a stupor, or, in the event that a town was nearby, he would go off in search of women and song — wine he did not need to search for, as he made sure to always carry a generous supply.

On one such sojourn the younger brother was beset upon by a band of marauders who sprang from the bushes, beat him with staffs about the head and shoulders, and made off with his purse. Luckily, this was one rare instance when the young profligate had the uncustomary foresight to give the better part of his money to his brother for safekeeping, so all he suffered on that occasion was a minor financial loss, a slightly blackened eye, and a mild case of wounded pride. Luck was with him also on another evening when a jealous husband, a blacksmith by trade, with a lantern jaw and hammer fists, tripped on a cobblestone, thus allowing him the precious seconds he needed to make a clean escape.

A week passed and the better part of another. The halfway point was well behind them. The elder brother felt thoroughly invigorated. Not so the younger whose constant drunkenness and nightly bacchanalia were taking a heavy toll. Mornings were most difficult. He detested mornings to begin with, and at normal times he did his best to avoid them, often not rising until the sun's disagreeable glare had begun to wane in the evening sky. On the road, however, it was imperative to put in as many miles as possible during daylight hours.

Rather than admit to the adverse effects of his over-indulgence, the younger brother would always bravely rise at the elder's prodding, laugh off his aching head — though, indeed, it was a hollow laugh — and pretend that all was well. Thus, he would stoically sally forth with throbbing temples and squinty, dark-rimmed, bloodshot eyes, a dull ache in the pit of his stomach, and a sour aftertaste left over from the previous evening's revelry that often would linger through most of the day.

As might be expected, the younger brother soon tired of this facade and so he was greatly pleased and relieved when a fierce storm struck one evening at a time when they happened to be in sight of a rustic, though agreeable-looking village inn, which would, he hoped, afford him a quiet room, a hot bath, and a chance to recuperate from the past fortnight's dissipation. His expectations, however, proved ill-founded. When the two brothers inquired as to the availability of lodgings, the innkeeper, though seemingly sympathetic, informed them that several other travelers before them had sought shelter from the storm, the result being that every room was taken. After seeing the younger's debilitated condition, though, the innkeeper did offer, for a modest sum, to set up two cots in a corner of the room that was used by the inn's patrons for eating and imbibing alcoholic beverages.

While in no sense an ideal situation, the brothers considered the cold, wet alternative and accepted the innkeeper's offer, the elder thinking that perhaps fate had brought him here with the object of furthering his spiritual education, the younger having no thoughts whatsoever other than to rest his aching head and weary bones. While he was loathe to admit it, the younger brother was feeling more flushed, feverish, and utterly wretched with every passing minute and wanted nothing more than to sink into oblivion.

Ruddy, rowdy, rotund, Brueghel-like figures crammed the smoke-drenched dining room. Townsfolk, farmers, peasants, and travelers, they were, talking, smoking, drinking, laughing, all of them seemingly intent upon making as much noise, while consuming as much as was humanly possible. These were the younger brother's kind of people, and on any other night he would have joined the festivities, but on this particular evening the very sight of so much gusto was enough to cause his head to spin and his stomach to do lazy cartwheels in sympathy.

While the innkeeper and his wife were setting up two cots in a shaded corner of the room, three of the patrons, thick of hand and of girth, called over to the brothers in drink-thickened voices, offering to buy them a drink. The brothers smiled politely, waved across the noisy, smoke-filled room while patting their lumpy, hay-filled mattresses, as if to say, 'thanks but no thanks,' and the thick men resumed their drinking.

At the younger's request, the elder took the cot nearest the wall, while the younger occupied the one closest to the night's cacophonous proceedings — the younger's logistics being based on the possibility that his dizzy head and churning stomach might give him cause to effectuate a hasty retreat out of the thick, unpainted, weathered-hardwood door. Thus, they settled in, as best they could, to sleep.

The elder brother had, apparently, not the least difficulty getting to sleep. Only minutes later, when the younger groaned to him about the noise and the smoke, the elder, who was facing the wall, snoozed heavily in reply. For the younger, however, sleep was as illusive as a swarm of fruit flies — that is to say it was not easy to catch hold of. The din, the smoke, and the laughter, seemed, in his increasingly feverish condition, to be conspiring against him. The smoke, the mirth, the din and cacophonous clatter seemed to be mocking him, twisting his ears, prying open his sweat glands, stirring up the vat of vinegar soup in his stomach while drilling pin-size holes in the sides of his head to release the resulting fumes. The evening's revelry seemed, at times, to be going on right inside his skull, his nerve endings, and in the very marrow of his bones. At other times, the babel of voices no longer seemed human, but like the barking of a kennel full of rabid strays. He tossed and twisted, stirring restlessly for an hour, maybe two, before those yelping hounds of hell dragged him, kicking and screaming into fitful, though blessed, insensibility.

About that time it dawned upon the three thick-set revelers, who had earlier asked the brothers to share a drink with them, that perhaps the two strangers had refused them not out of simple fatigue, as their motions had seemed to suggest. Instead, perhaps, their refusal to drink with them, one of the thicksters suggested, might have been the result of just plain high-and-mightiness. Perhaps, added another, in the coarsest imaginable language, they thought themselves too good to drink with three men who made their living by the sweat of their brows and the strength of their backs and hands. In no time, the brothers' simple gesture of refusal, in the hazy brains of the three musclebound drunkards, had been blown all out of proportion, taking on the dimensions of a hard slap across the face. Nay, worse, an insult to their manhood! Nay, more serious even than that, a curse on their grandmothers' graves! At all events, this was exactly the sort of effrontery that no self-respecting oaf could, in good conscience, take sitting down.

With this in mind, the three ample-waisted, ruddy-faced drunkards arose laboriously from their overburdened chairs and wobbled over to have a closer look and the two insolent toplofty snobs who had the temerity to judge good men based upon the sketchiest evidence. Whereupon they loudly cursed the audacity and belittled the manhood of those who would spurn and then rudely sleep through such a glorious festival of over-indulgence as they, out of the goodness of their hearts, had offered to share with these two sleeping ingrates.

Being that the younger brother's cot was positioned nearest them, it was he upon whom the brutes started beating. A hand must have instinctively leapt out as he was waking and struck one of his attackers quite forcibly on the cheek — at least that was one of the complaints lodged against him as they hauled him from his bed, still half asleep, and commenced to push him around and then to slap him and then to pummel him with blows to his body and his undefended face and head.

As for the possibility of extricating himself, there was

none. As for reasoning with them, that too was impossible. His protests fell on deaf ears. As for why they were doing this, he had not the slightest idea. All he did know was that three vaguely familiar brutes with hot, stale breath, scowling red-veined faces, and anvils where their hands should have been, were beating him half senseless for no apparent reason. Worse, his fever and depleted condition gave him neither the strength nor the conviction to give back even half so good as he was getting. So, there he was, poor fellow, hardly able to defend himself, and without even the benefit of his customary instinct for self-preservation — which under normal circumstances was quite considerable.

Fortunately, for the sake of our young casualty, the innkeeper intervened to mediate on his behalf before the brutes had damaged him too seriously. This act of sensible interposition, however, was hastily nullified by other deeds which were, to the victim's way of thinking, outright travesties. Instead of having the louts arrested, as the owner of any respectable establishment would have done, or at very least treating the drunkards to a bum's rush into the cold night, instead the innkeeper verily coddled the thugs and called them all by name! Instead of a swift kick into rainy oblivion, he gently chided the drunken brawlers in a tone that carried no more indignity than one would use on an errant child who had purposefully spilled a glass of milk. Was it not an outrage? Here he was, simply ushering the ruffians back to their table, leaving the battered victim with nothing but an apology for what was euphemistically termed "the inconvenience!"

Contempt gave way to bitterness, pain to self pity as the younger brother sat on the lumpy mattress and nursed his wounds. He had a split lip, a lump on his head, possibly a cracked rib, or worse, and his attackers were back at their seats, ordering another round, and being treated as if they had created no more than a minor annoyance. Where was the fairness in this world? Where was the justice?

And where had his brother been while all this was going on? Hard though it was to imagine, the man had been, and still was, deep in slumber! Dead to the world! Sleeping like a statue! Why does one not travel alone, he angrily wondered, if not for sake of having one's traveling companions there for protection? A wave of incoherence suddenly came crashing over the rocky shore of his inner being, causing him to conclude, unreasonably, that somehow his sleeping brother was to blame. Whereupon, he leaned over and shook the elder roughly.

The elder awoke to a barrage of harsh criticism for not having risen to the younger's defence. Seeing his brother's condition, of course, he felt only sympathy for his brother and not the slightest contempt. Indeed, his compassion grew more empathetic with each passing affront and insult. And nor did he make any attempt to defend himself against the tirade — for the poor man had obviously reached his breaking point. Finally, with quite words of comfort, he managed to calm the younger down, and to convince him that he should try to go back to sleep. The younger agreed to this suggestion in principle, but fearing a repeat performance by the brutes, he asked that the elder switch beds with him. And as many a loving brother would have done under similar circumstance, the elder more than gladly complied. Be not mistaken as to the nature of the motivations of those who aspire to become *zaddikim*. While it may be true that a zaddik does not shy away from life's hardships and uncertainties, and it is true that he denies bodily comfort, he does so not out of some masochistic yearning, but for the purpose of achieving the greater pleasure that can be derived by completing the soul's cycle of correction. Thus the elder welcomed the opportunity to place himself between the thugs and his errant brother, but not because he had any desire to have the stuffing beaten out of him. If, however, his body did receive a pummeling —well so be it! Certainly, it would be for a reason. Perhaps some wrong deed in a previous life demanded retribution. At all events, he would accept what fate or providence had in store, firm in the conviction that the pain suffered by his body would be serving a higher purpose, namely, the purification of his soul. And so it was that the two brothers traded places, and, eventually, they drifted off to sleep.

Sure enough, later in the evening, as fate would have it — or perhaps it was providence — it dawned upon one of the three thugs that they had attacked only one of the impudent strangers, while sparing the other. This, in his inebriated judgment, did not seem equitable. Both were guilty of the same holier-than-thou impudence. Both had demonstrated equal conceit by refusing to share drink with them. Should they not, then, he asked his companions, mete out equal treatment to the other? The brutes agreed. In good conscience, they could not beat upon only one of the haughty newcomers and let the other off scot free. Justice demanded that the other receive equal retribution. The incident, long forgotten by the brothers, in the benumbed brains of the three brutes, had become a matter of honor, principle and integrity. There was no question that the other traveler, too, would have to be punched, kicked, and viciously cudgeled. Fair, after all, was only fair.

The brutes rose from their seats and lumbered over to the shadowed corner in which the two brothers were sleeping, both of them facing the wall. The thugs, of course, had no idea that the two brothers had switched beds, so quite naturally it was the man who was sleeping in the bed closest to the wall who was the target of their animosity. As it turned out, the ruffians did at least possess a grain of decency. Thinking that the man closest to them had already received his comeuppance, they took great pains not to disturb him. And that is how the younger brother came to be dragged out of bed a second time and given a thorough thrashing, while the elder slept like a newborn babe.

A strange sensation overcame the younger brother as his body was suffering that second attack. Attribute it to fever, if you will, sickness, a concussion, or merely the utter absurdity of the situation, but he hardly felt the blows that were hailing upon him from all sides and angles. Whatever the cause, he was suddenly catapulted into an exquisite state of awareness, higher, purer, more lucid by far than any he had previously imagined. In those moments of mystical recognition his life came into clear and perfect focus. The facade of illusion with which he had always protected himself began to crack and then to crumble, leaving him alone with the naked reality of his empty existence. He saw it all: the futility of his hedonism and ribaldry, the price of his physical dissipation, and the true agony of his moral decay.

Those few seconds of mystical revelation taught him more than a lifetime of self-indulgence. And to whom did he owe this transformation if not the brutes? He laughed! How he laughed! Which, as it happened, did much toward lessening the severity of the beating. So uproarious did his laughter become that the oafs lost the thread of their concentration and became confused and disoriented. Little pleasure can be derived, even of the most brutal and vulgar kind, from striking a defenseless madman — especially one who takes pleasure in the beating!

The elder brother awoke to the sound of laughter — not just that of his brother, but others had also been bitten by the mirthful contagion, including the brutes, themselves! At that moment, he too underwent something of a transformation, for he understood what had happened and immediately realized that indeed fate, or some power higher than themselves had guided them to this inn on this rain-swept night.

The two brothers never did complete their journey to the city. They had no need to. In that one evening, they had transcended any further need for restless wandering and the visceral agonies that pass for worldly experiences. And so it was that they returned to their village — two brothers who had become zaddiks. They lived long, productive, loving lives in the village and through the years many seekers traveled from far and wide to request their counsel or simply to pay respects.

In their later years, the two wise zaddiks would sometimes recall with fondness the night in the village inn, and remember the two beatings which the younger had suffered at the hands of those three brutes. And, as always, they would smile, bless the brutes, and thank them in their evening prayers.

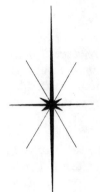

# 21

## *Victim of Circumstance*

A COMMON EXCUSE FOR FAILING TO LIVE UP TO ONE'S FULL potential is often stated with words to the effect that one has to make a living. Certainly, everyone must earn his keep in this world and everyone has an obligation to do all that one can to maintain and improve the living conditions of his or her family. Yet, this concept of "making a living" can be used to conceal or otherwise excuse a multitude of responsibilities, spiritual, emotional, and intellectual.

"A man's got to make a living." What is the habitual

user of this old chestnut really saying if not ... it's out of my hands... it's not my fault... I'm a victim of circumstances? The very words *make a living* seem to denote something that is one step removed from living. In fact, it might be said that one whose energy is completely taken up in the making and not the living is not really living at all.

The concept of making a living can hide a multitude of emotional insecurities. It can be used as justification for a stock broker or other professional person to work ninety hours a week and rarely see his or her family. It can give one a reason to remain in a job that is neither enjoyable nor challenging. It can allow one to be obstinate and unforgiving, and absolve one for being complacent and emotionally unresponsive.

Did the Emanator place us here to engage exclusively in hand-to-mouth survival? Is material acquisition a fitting foundation on which to build a life? Are we merely slaves to the system, gears in government, corporate, or religious machinery, cogs in wheels of Progress? Is life nothing more than a string of days for mindlessly, dutifully trudging through? Kabbalah teaches that there is no such thing as a victim of circumstances — if we are victims it is of our own minds, our own patterns of thinking and perceiving. There is no empirical criterion by which to determine success or failure. The value of a person is internal and cannot be measured solely by his or her position or monetary worth.

An old parable tells of a holy man named Yohan, who earned his living as a cobbler. It is said that so completely had Yohan transcended Desire to Receive for Oneself Alone that to wear his shoes was to feel shoeless, as if one were walking on air. Many people wondered why a man of such obvious gifts chose to remain a humble shoemaker, but Yohan had transcended his work entirely, transforming what for others appeared to be a menial task into an endeavor of the highest spiritual order.

According to the kabbalistic teachings, past incarnations determine the amount of desire possessed by each of us. We are born with a certain degree of longing that does not increase or diminish throughout each lifetime, but, regardless, the desire one is born with is always sufficient to meet one's spiritual needs. People who are born with a greater degree of desire have more spiritual ground to make up, so to speak, and therefore feel compelled to excel, to accomplish more than others. The reason that certain individuals who are born with blazing desires fail to achieve their full potential, while others who are born with comparatively little desire prosper, emotionally, spiritually, and financially, lies in the ability of the person with the lesser desire to transform Desire to Receive for Oneself Alone into Desire to Receive for the Sake of Sharing.

The true measure of a person's worth lies not in the magnitude of his or her inborn desire, but in how positively or negatively one implements his or her inherent aspirations. No amount of ambition, if it is rooted in the negative aspect of desire can lead one to spiritual fulfillment. However, by transforming the negative aspect of desire into the positive aspect, work can then have the opposite effect of challenging a person to reach his or her full spiritual, emotional, and intellectual potential.

Thus, to the kabbalist's way of thinking, the choice between Desire to Receive for Oneself Alone and Desire to Receive for the Sake of Sharing is reduced to one of absurd simplicity. For whereas the person who is immersed totally in Desire for Oneself Alone will never be satisfied in his or her work, the person who can transform Desire to Receive for Oneself Alone into Desire to Receive for the Sake of Sharing will find fulfillment in almost any non-violent occupation. And while those who are motivated by the negative aspect of desire can expect nothing more than material acquisition; those, on the other hand, who are motivated by the positive aspect of desire can transcend negativity and achieve Infinite contentment.

What is love?

This question elicits as many responses as there are people who care to formulate a response. Kabbalistically speaking there are only two kinds of love, illusionary and real, false and true. Let us examine the former for in this world it is by far the more prevalent.

> False love is jealous.
> False love tells lies.
> False love is smug.
> False love is boastful.
> False love pays lip service.
> False love is insecure.
> False love deceives.
> False love is greedy.
> False love makes demands.
> False love clings.
> False love smothers.
> False love is guilty.
> False love "turns me on".
> False love is placed on pedestals.
> False love is paid for with dead mink.

False love divorces.
False love complains.
False love is convenient.
False love looks out for number one.
False love reads like a grocery list:
DWF 35 sincere, slinky, svelte & sensual,
seeks financially secure, upwardly-mobile
prof.
DWM, tall, drk, hndsm, 6 ft.+/yacht/
muscles/object mtrimny.
False love runs on empty.
False love is hate.

As illusive as a sub atomic tendency, as cranky as a
wounded bear, as complicated as a Mack truck's transmission
— false love eludes, frightens, and confuses us. True love is
sublimely simple, for unlike false love which has many
desires, real love has but one aspiration: To Share.


## Lack

Kabbalah teaches that we lack nothing, that any
deficiency we may experience is an illusion derived from the
lower seven, the creative process of the Line. Does this mean
that sadness is non-existent? — that anger, confusion,
desperation, the great chasm that separates us from ourselves
and from others, are all just figments of unreality? In a word,
yes. According to Kabbalah, the Infinite aspect of existence,
and hence of humanity, the First Three, is totally fulfilled.
The lack we feel, the emptiness and alienation, the anger, the
greed and envy, are aspects of the Line, and the Line, as we
have determined, is an illusion which was caused by the
Tsimtsum and manifested in the lower seven of the Line.

The Creator's only aspiration is to share Endless beneficence. It was we, the emanated, who demanded free will sufficient to alleviate Bread of Shame. The reason we feel unfulfilled is that Line transfers the illusion of space, the gap inherent in the lower seven, to our Infinite Encircling Vessels, the Head or First Three. The only reason we think we are not fulfilled is not because the ten vessels of the Circles the Infinite aspect of existence are unrevealed, but rather that the creative process of the line creates a consciousness of depravation within the circular vessels, but only from the perspective of the Line.

The challenge faced by the kabbalist is to redirect his or her consciousness from the lower seven and raise it to the level of the upper three. Lack exists only in the world of illusion. Failure to restrict causes an individual to remain in the illusionary realm. Through the practice of positive resistance the kabbalist transcends the negative aspect of the Curtain and rises to a state of consciousness that is impervious to the illusion presented by the lower seven, the "Body" of the Line.

The separation of the three from the seven was the primary qualification for the establishment of creation, for without the aspect of voluntary restriction we would have no way of removing Bread of Shame. Such is the nature of the paradox that it is only by confronting reality in the manner that the negative pole in a light bulb defies the electricity sent toward it, or the mirror reflects the image before it, that Light is brought into this world. Reality, the Circular and Infinite aspect of existence, must remain hidden to allow us the opportunity for correction. The constant sense of depravation, the personal and cultural alienation experienced by so many people in this world of unremitting stress and friction is a product of the Line, the illusion, but like any illusion it pales, cowers and finally surrenders when confronted by the face of Supreme Reality in the manner that darkness is always defeated when challenged by light.

From the perspective of the higher realms of awareness lack does not exist. When one has risen above the illusionary state of consciousness the negative babble of this world of resistance becomes like the distant squabbling of geese and ducks, interesting possibly, but seldom engaging emotionally. Yet, the fact that the kabbalist disconnects totally with this unreal world should not be taken to mean that he or she runs away or hides from negativity. It is not necessary to become a recluse or withdraw physically from society and civilization to transcend negative existence. Rather it is by confronting the darkness that the Light is revealed. The kabbalist meets reality, so to speak, head on, face to face, for it is through resistance that the Light is brought out of hiding. Thus does the kabbalist rise above the illusion of lack that is both the boon and the bane of humanity (in the sense that it tortures us while at the same time offering us the opportunity for correction) to again defeat the paradox and lift from his or her shoulders the negativity that is the burden of this realm.

## Amnesia

Let us briefly examine the cause of lapses in memory and the constant interruptions that break the continuity of our daily lives. Why do we lose our train of thought? Why do we go off on wild tangents in our conversations? Why must we put up with a constant stream of petty disturbances? Why are we subject to sudden mood swings that can take us from bliss to sadness in a matter of seconds?

The answer is that the Line is continually exerting its influence into every aspect of our lives. The Line injects space, the gap, into everything we say and do. Were it not for the lower seven of the Line our lives would have total coherence. No longer would we be subject to trivial disturbances; no more would we have trouble seeing things through from beginning to end. However, as desirable this may sound, total continuity would completely obscure and negate the very purpose of our existence which is, of course, the removal of Bread of Shame.

**Limitation**

Man cannot cause chaos in upper (inner) levels of his own or of cosmic experience. Fortunately, the negative activity of man does not reach beyond the level of Malkhut. He can, however, wreck havoc in the seven of the Line. Only Malkhut is subject to Desire to Receive for the Self Alone. Through restriction we convert the negative aspect of desire into the positive aspect and thus tap into the state of consciousness which is above and beyond the realm of illusion.

The vacuum created at the time of the Tsimtsum caused the illusion of the Line to descend without interruption. Thus, from the finite (illusionary) perspective, there is an empty space between each of the ten Circular sefirot which is imparted to the Circles by the Line, but there is no such gap between the ten sefirot of the Line which begin from the Endless and extend unobstructed to the Middle Point of Malkhut.

The Line, in other words, is a total illusion and thus the

gap in the Circles is itself illusionary. However, from our
finite perspective, it is the Line that appears real while the
Circle seems to be illusionary.

There is total continuity between the First Three of the
Line and all ten sefirot of Circles. Only from our finite
perspective does the illusion appear to be real. The seven of
the Line causes all of our problems and difficulties, chaos and
disorder, but the moment we inject conscious, voluntary
restriction into the equation we remove the illusion and
reveals the Light. This occurs not only in the normal process
of the First Three, which automatically reveals Light because
there is no Curtain in the Circles, but also in the seven of the
Line which are obscured by a Curtain.

We must remember that while the physical universe is
effected by whether or not we are converting the negative
aspect of desire into the positive, nevertheless there is a
certain component of the universal order which we have
absolutely no control over. While we are certainly capable of
molding, shaping, even transforming, the illusion of the lower
seven, nothing we do has the slightest effect on the infinite
reality of the upper First Three.

Above Malkhut negativity is capable of no influence, for
the illusion which is darkness can never exist in the presence
of the all embracing Light. By injecting the aspect of
restriction we create affinity with the Light, thus obliterating
the illusion of darkness within the Circular sefirot and also in
the seven of the Line.

Negative activity has no effect on the man or woman who
has converted Desire to Receive for the Self Alone into
Desire to Receive for the Sake of Sharing. By connecting with

our Infinite aspect we reveal the Light, whereas a failure to exercise restriction causes us to remain submerged in spiritual darkness and limitation.

## On Becoming Unreasonable

Maimonides whose "Mishnah Torah" (Copy of the Law) was the first systematic exposition of Jewish Law, whose "articles of faith" are quoted in most Jewish prayer books, whose main philosophical work "Morah Nevukhim" (Guide for the Perplexed) strongly influenced all philosophical thinking of his era, and whose "Yad ha-Hazakah" (Strong Hand) restructured the entire content of the Bible, was obviously a man possessed of remarkable reasoning capabilities. Yet, he once compared himself seemingly unfavorably with the Greek philosopher Aristotle saying that Aristotle's deductive logic far exceeded his own. In fact this seeming compliment carried more than a shadow of irony, for actually Maimonides considered the rational mind to be an impediment to true awareness, meaning that while from the terrestrial perspective Aristotle's reasoning capacity may have been greater than his own, speaking from a celestial level (the First Three) it was Maimonides whose mental acuity was superior.

Albert Einstein, also indisputably a man of tremendous analytical endowments and rational cognizance, frequently credited leaps of intuition with his greatest discoveries and mental breakthroughs. "To imagine is everything", he is often quoted as saying, and "the gift of fantasy has meant more to me than my talent for absorbing positive knowledge." Later in life, however, Einstein took an intransigent position with regard quantum mechanics. His total inability to accept certain precepts of quantum theory, so infuriated Neils Bohr, the Father of Quantum Mechanics, that the latter would later accuse Einstein of no longer thinking, but of just being rational.

The rational, reasoning mind accounts for but a minuscule fragment of our true mental potential. Contrary to what is believed by most Western educators who place great emphasis on mindless regurgitation of rote-learned facts, tests, grades, and IQ examinations (all of which are concerned only with the rational mind) by far the greater measure of human mental aptitude rests hidden, clothed in darkness, dormant and unrevealed until such time as the higher realms of consciousness are aroused and re-illuminated through a continuing attitude of positive resistance.

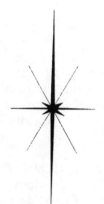

# Post-Script

## *I'll take the High Road ...*

TWO FORCES EXERT INFLUENCE ON HUMANITY. TWO energy-intelligences, positive and negative, battle constantly for dominance over the minds and hearts of man. The positive aspect we will call "the high road," from the old Scottish folk song, and, accordingly, the negative aspect we will give the name "the low road." They are two roads, yet one. The same, yet different.

Getting to the low road is a proverbial breeze. Unlike the high road, the low road is wide, smooth — a freeway — or so it seems. Certainly, of the two roads, the low road is the more well-traveled. One can coast down the low road, secure in the knowledge that he or she will never be alone. The vast majority of people choose the seeming comfort and convenience of the low road, little knowing that what appears at first to be the easier way inevitably proves in the long run to be the more arduous and demanding.

Being elevated, the high road remains out of sight, above the range of the senses, invisible to the naked eye. One must therefore have a certain sense of adventure, faith, and optimism before embarking upon the high road, a feeling that something positive will result from the long uphill climb. The high road is the path of the sefirotic triumvirate known to Kabbalah as the Head or First Three. The First Three, synonymous with the soul, must remain obscured from common view. Otherwise, we would revert back to the condition before the Tsimtsum with no way of ridding ourselves of Bread of Shame.

When the Emanator restricted to allow for the emergence of free will and its faithful associate, Desire to Receive, necessity dictated that the high road be an uphill climb. At the Tsimtsum, when the Endless imparted free will to the emanated creations, It initiated a situation whereby human energy-intelligences would be obliged to choose between the high road, the positive path, and the low road, the negative. This, however, was not the will of the Emanator, but of the emanated. For as has been often repeated, the Emanator's only aspiration was, is, and will always be to share.

The Emanator has no intention other than to impart Endless benevolence. But as much as the Emanator desires to extend Light to the vessels, the souls of man, we cannot receive the Light in good conscience without relieving Bread of Shame. A gift imparts no joy to the giver if there is no one to receive it. There must be a vessel for the Light to be revealed.

Just as there is no light in the cold, dark reaches of space because the light has nothing there to reflect from, so to do the dark places in the consciousness of humanity remain in darkness until positive resistance is exercised. Conscious, positive resistance is the mediating principle between the high road and the low road, the positive and negative aspects of our existence. Resistance reveals Light which obliterates darkness. The paradox is that by resisting the Light, the gift we most desire, we receive, but by accepting it — like the darkness it envelops the sunlight, allowing it no opportunity for revealment —we too remain in spiritual darkness unless and until we exercise resistance and thereby alleviate Bread of Shame.

The high road is there always, quietly impelling us to resist the negative pull of the lower seven, which is a constant in this finite World of Restriction, and to choose instead to walk in the Light of the infinite First Three. Of course, in the Infinite sense, the high road is the only road. In the long term, it is path that we will all one day follow. In the short term, however, when we are speaking only of life in this finite world, the low road is by far the most frequently taken. The choice is ours. The high road leads to truth, the low road to illusion. The high road leads to sublime contentment, the low road to hardship and worry. Those who choose the high road walk in Light, those who choose the low road have darkness as their constant companion.

# Kabbalistic Terminology

# KABBALISTIC TERMINOLOGY

**ABSOLUTE FARNESS** — The condition resulting when a change of form is so great as to become an opposition of form.

**ASCENT** — Purification. The purer is higher, the impure (thicker) is lower.

**BEGINNING OF EXTENSION** — The Root of all extension of Light. Also called Crown.

**BINDER** — The Kingdom of an Upper Sefira becomes the Crown of a lower thus each Kingdom "binds" every upper Sefira with the one below.

**BINDING** — The enclosing of the 10 Sefirot of the Head in the 10 Sefirot of the Returning Light.

**BINDING BY STRIKING** — The action of the Curtain which repels the Light and hinders it from entering the fourth phase.

**BOUNDARY** — The Curtain at each level stretches out and makes a "Boundary."

**CAUSE** — That which brings about the revelation of a level.

**CONCLUSION** — The fourth phase.

**CORPOREALITY** — Anything perceived by the five senses.

**CROWN** — The purest of all levels. Keter.

**CURTAIN** — The power of future restriction (additional to that of the Tsimtsum) which prevents Light from entering the fourth phase.

**DESCENT** — Impurification. Descent from a level. Thickening.

**DRAWN** — The descent of Light brought about by the power of longing (impurity) in the Emanation is said to be "drawn" down.

**EMERGENCE TO THE EXTERIOR** — A change in the form of Spiritual Substance.

**ENCIRCLING** — That which brings about the revelation of a level is said to surround or encircle that level.

**ERECT HEIGHT** — When the Lights of the Head are clothed in the Vessel of the Head we speak of the Countenance as being of "erect height."

**ESSENCE** — The Light of Wisdom is the Essence and "life" of an Emanation.

**FAR** — An extensive change in form.

**FROM ABOVE TO BELOW** — "Straight Light" extending in the Vessels from higher to lower (purer to impure) levels is described as descending "from above to below."

**FROM BELOW TO ABOVE** — "Returning Light" drawn in order of levels from lower to higher (impure to purer) is described as ascending "from below to above."

**GROUND or FLOOR** — The Kingdom of each level or world is termed the ground or floor of that level or world.

**HEAD** — The three Sefirot of the Upper Light.

**HEAD** — The nine Sefirot of the Upper Light which extend by Binding by Striking on the Curtain of Kingdom.

**ILLUMINATION FROM AFAR** — Light which is unable to enter the Sefirot but surrounds it from a distance.

**INDIVIDUAL** — Light clothed in the Sefira of the Crown.

**INNER LIGHT** — The Light inside each Sefira.

**IN PASSING** — Each Sefira contains two kinds of Light, the Light which is indigenous to it, and the Light which is left there when the Light of the Endless passes through it. The latter is said to remain there in "passing."

**IMPURITY** — A strong Desire to Receive. "Thickness."

**INTELLIGENCE** — Reflection on the ways of cause and effect in order to clarify the final result.

**JUNCTURE** — Equivalence of form between two Spiritual Substances.

**KINGDOM** — The last phase. The tenth and final sefira from Keter in which the greatest Desire to Receive is manifested and in which all correction takes place. Malkhut. The physical world.

**LENGTH** — The distance from the purest phase to the impurest phase.

**LIFE** — Light which is received from the next highest level and not from the Endless, is called Light of Life or Female Light.

**LINE** — The Light found in the Vessels of Straightness. Also denotes finitude.
**LIVING** — The Light of Wisdom.

**MATERIAL** — The impurity in the Countenance from the fourth phase of Desire. Analogous to physical matter.

**NEAR** — Closeness of one form to another.

**NOT JOINED** — Changes in forms causes them to be "not joined" to one another.

**NULLIFIED** — When two spiritual substances are equal in form they return to one substance, the smaller being "nullified" by the larger.

**ONE WITHIN THE OTHER** — An outer Circle is defined as the cause of the Circle within it. One Within the Other points to a relationship of cause and effect.

**OUTER** — The purer part of each Vessel is distinguished as the "outer" which is illuminated by surrounding Light from afar.

**PASSING** — The Light that passes through the sefirot is called "passing" Light.

**PIPE** — Vessels of Straightness are termed "Pipes" since they draw and confine the Light within themselves as a pipe confines the water which passes through it.

**PRIMORDIAL MAN** — The first World. Also called a Single Line. The root of the phase of man in this world.

**PURIFICATION OF THE CURTAIN** — Purification of the impurity in the fourth phase brought about in direct proportion to the Desire to Receive.

**RETURNING LIGHT** — Light which is prevented from entering any world by the Curtain.

**ROOF** — The Crown at each level: true for both Sefirot and Worlds.

**SOUL** — The Light clothed in the Vessel of Intelligence.

**SPIRIT** — The Light clothed in the Vessel of the Small Face.

**SPIRITUAL** — Devoid of material attributes, place, time and shape.

**STRAIGHT** — The descent of the Upper Light to the impure Vessels of the fourth phase is described as being "straight". Compare the swift "straight" descent of a falling stone with the slow meandering descent of a falling feather. The Earth's gravity (Desire to Receive) exerts a more direct influence on the stone. In a similar manner do the Vessels of Straightness, whose longing is strong, cause Light to descend swiftly in a "Straight" line.

**SURROUNDING LIGHT** — The Light which surrounds each Sefira, the illumination of which is received from the En Sof "at a distance."

**THE ENDLESS** — The source of the Vessels of the Circles.

**THE FIRST THREE** — The first three Sefirot: Crown, Wisdom, and Intelligence. Also called the Head of the Countenance.

**THE LARGE FACE** — The Countenance of the Crown in the World of Emanation, its essence is the light of Wisdom.

**THE PURPOSE OF ALL OF THIS** — The fourth phase of the fourth phase.

**THE SMALL FACE** — Six Sefirot of the third phase whose essence is the Light of Mercy, containing illumination from Wisdom without its essence.

**WATERS OF LIGHT** — Light which descends from its level.

**WHEEL** — The Sefirot of Circles.

**WISDOM** — Knowledge of the final ends of all aspects of reality.

**Z' 'T, THE SEVEN LOWER SEFIROT** — The seven Sefirot; Mercy, Judgment, Beauty, Lasting Endurance, Majesty, Foundation and Kingdom,comprising the Body of the Countenance.

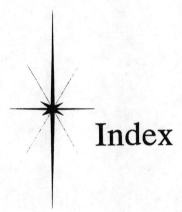

# Index

# Index

## — A —

Abraham, 40
Act of awareness, 145,148
Act of Creation, 145,149
Advertizing, 55
Age of Aquarius, 25,27
Age of Darkness, 28
Age of Enlightenment, 28,
    29, 33
Age of Light, 28
Alchemists, 159
Alien spacecraft, 28
Alleviation, 41
Alteration of
    consciousness, 40,
    117
Altered States, 54,55,57
Alternate Universes, 67
Altruism, 25
Ambiguity, 94
America, 64
Amnesia, 223
Apocalypse, 28,29,32
Archimedes, 64
Ari, the, 80,81,82,84,85,
    125,126,131,132,137,
    138,139,180,182
Aristotle, 61,226
Ashlag, Rabbi, 189
Astral Influences, 40
Astral Projection, 41
Atomic Level 41,42
Atomic Structure, 85
Awareness, 31,124

## — B —

Backward in Time, 21
Beautiful Illusion, 62
Beauty, 112,113,114,125,
    127, 129
Beginning, Middle and End,
    27
Bible, 32
Biblical writings, 32
Binah, 80,83,98,99,100,
    102,103,104,112,126,
    128,136,163,166
Binah's Exertion, 103
Binah's Light, 103
Binah's Nature, 100
Binding by Striking, 80,
    130,143,144
Bio-rhythms, 20
Biological, social and
    cultural, 29
Birth, Growth and Death,
    163
Birth of Desire, the, 90
Birth, Life and Death, 23
Black Holes, 20,67
Blessings of Hokhmah, 96
Bohr, Neils, 227
Book of Formation, the, 120
Brainstorm, 102
Brainwashing, 65
Bread of Shame, 28,31,57,
    74,88,90,99,111,107,
    116,125,126,129,138,
    148,149,160,163,168,

171,172,179,182,184,
188,203,222,224,230,
231
Bureaucrats, 55

— C —

Candlemaker, the, 191-197
Cartesian paradigm, 35-37,
39,42
Cause and Effect, 43,86,97
Celestial bodies, 40
Central Column, 141,142
Channels for the Light, 64
Chaos, 30
Charity, 74,67
Chasm of Illusion, 98
Chemical corruption, 46
Chemical dependency, 48,49
Circle of the Endless, 73
Circle of Endlessness, 160
Circle of Infinity, 161
Circle of Keter, 130
Circles, the, 82,128,135,
145
Circuit of Energy, 116
Circular Concept, 75
Circular Condition, 22
Circular Sefira, 136,127
Circular Vessels, 108,125,
126,136,137,163
Circular World, 81
Collective Consciousness,
26,29

Columbus, Christopher, 64,16
Comfort, 69
Communication, 63
Compassionate soul, 30
Complacency, 67,69
Computer, 30
Concentric Cirles 112
Concentric Circles
(illustration), 128
Connecting Link, 94
Consciousness, the, 27,29,
33,57,63,84,99,101,
113,116,118,119
Corporeal Illusion, 31
Corrective Process, 68,163
Cosmic awareness, 69,116
Cosmic blueprint, 28
Cosmic Code, 32
Cosmic process, 31
Creation, (prerequisite),
106
Creative Illusion, 160
Creative Process, the, 81,
97,111
Creator, the, 90,126,131,
132
Crown, the, 113,114,129
Crude Spirit, 125
Curie, Pierre, 63
Curtain, the, 66,80,81,
90,120,124,128,131,
143
Cycle of correction, 27,
30,36

**— D —**

Dark side of the Curtain, 83
Darkness, 27,30,33
Death of the illusion, 187
Death of Moses, 188-189
Death, 41
Deprivation, 108
Descartes, Rene, 37
Desire to Receive, 28, 55-57,64,68,69,73, 74,80,83,85,88,89, 90,97,100,101,102, 104,105,106,107,110, 112,113,116,119,126, 129,136,145,147,148, 152,164-166,168,169, 171,172,176,185,187, 188,178,179,200,202, 203,204,218,219,224, 225
Desire to Share, 89, 98, 100,102,104
Determinism, 148
Dimension, 80
Discomfort, 41,44,69
Divine Light, 104
DNA of consciousness, 28
Drawn to the end, 86
Dream walk, 52
Drugs (addiction), 45,46, 49
(cure), 49
(legalize), 51
(rehabilitation), 49
(why?), 52

**— E —**

Early man, 52
Earthly conception, 36
Ecological balance, 30
Edison, Thomas 63
Educational system, 55
Einstein, 21,60-63,226
Einstein's theories, 31
Electron, 42
Electronic Age, 65
Emanation of the Light, 113
Emanator, the, 90,112, 113,131,132,218
Emotional, 90
Empirical validation, 43
En Sof, 26,73,111,132, 147,161,162,177
Encircling Vessels, 54, 68,107,127,145,161, 222
Endless, the, 23,69,81, 97,114,125
Endless abundance, 91
Endless Illumination, 79, 81
Endless Light, 115,130
Endless peace, 29,175,176

Endless reality, 156
Endurance, 112
Energy-force, 94
Energy and Matter, 31,84
Energy-Intelligence, 22,
    28,29,63,64,73,88,
    89,94,98-101,107,
    116,124,137,142,157
England, 51
Environmental protection,
    48
Essence of all desire, 90
Essence of Reality, 137
Eternal damnation, 32
Ether winds, 62
Evil, 57,110
Evil inclinations, 57
Evolution, 29,67,113
Exertions, 112
Existence, 29,56,66,115
Existence or Non-existence,
    21
Explores, 63

— F —

Fable of two Brothers, the,
    204-216
Faces of Evil, 56
Face of Desire, 56
Fantasy world, 118
Fear of Flying, 66
Featureless ground state,
    30

Feminine, 112
Filament, the, 145
Final Emendation, 31
Finite body, the, 124
Finite Existence, 30
Finite nature, 156
Finite vessels, 88
First Three, the, 20,
    22,41,68,69,83,97,
    104,115,123,124,
    127,129,130,135,
    136,139,163,166,
    167,221,222,225,
    230
First Act of Creation, 74
Force, the, 131
Forces of Restriction, 94
Foundation, 112
Four Phases, the, 112-114,
    136
Fourth Phase, 80,81
Free will, 110,148
Fuller, R. Buckminster,
    158

— G —

Gamma ray, 42
Gevura, 103
Giving, 71
Global Village, the, 154
Good over bad, 33
Grade of will, 100
Gravity, 20,67-69,85

Great Beyond, 28
Great Discoveries, 63
Great Mystery, the, 29
Great Social Upheavals, 25,
26
Growth, 162

— H —

Happiness, 75
Harmony, 25,158
Head of the Line, the, 130
Hell-Fire, 33
Hesed, 103
Higher Consciousness, 33,
55
Hod, 103
Hokhmah, 80,83,96,98,101,
102,103,104,112,128,
130,132,135,136,138,
163,166
Hokhmah's Light, 101
Holland, 51
Human Body, 68
Human Consciousness, 30
Human species, 27
Huxley, Aldous, 159
Hypnosis, 43
Hypnotic trance, 43
Hypocritical Laws, 49
Hysteria, 46

— I —

Illumination, 80,82,83,
101,130
Illusion, 29,54,56,60,66,
83,90,97,111,117,119,
123,124,139,148,152
Illusion of Concealment,
82
Illusion of Darkness, 127,
163,169
Illusion of lack, the, 84,
85
Illusionary separation,
81
Illusionary world, 86
Impurity, 81
India, 64
Infinite Encircling
Vessels, 97
Infinite Light, 124,116
Infinite perspective, 91
Infinite reality, 40,119
Infinity, 124
Inner Encircling Vessels,
97
Inner-space, 116
Intelligence, 98,112-114,
127,129
Interplanetary travel, 67
Inventors, 63
Involuntary, 87

— J —

Jeremiah, The Prophet, 27

Judgement, 112
Justice, 25

— K —

Kabbalah (Philosophy of),
  19,67
Kabbalistic believes, 19
Kabbalistic Wisdom, 29,32,
  36,43,163
Karmic correction, 66,
  153
Keter, 83,93,98,105,113,
  125,128,130,135,136,
  138,163,166
Keter (Light or Vessel),
  94
Keter vs. Malkhut, 109,
  110
King David, 27
Kingdom, the, 84,100,106,
  112-114,127
Klippot, 31,124,166

— L —

Lack, 221
Laser beams, 67
Law makers, 50,55
Law enforcement, 46
Laws of Science, 43
Lethal substances, 46
Levels of Circles, 181
Levels of consciousness,
  43,105

Life over death, 33
Life of crime, 49
Light, the, 30,31,56,66,
  79,80,84-87,89,90,
  91,99,100-102,105,
  110,112,113,119,
  129,132,190
Light of Endless, the, 82,
  98,100,101,103
Light of Hokhmah, 97,103
Light of Life, the, 81,
  126
Light of Mercy, 83,100-105,
  112,136
Light of Nefesh, 125,126
Light of Wisdom, 82,98,
  101-105
Light of the Circles, 81,
  126,181
Light of the Endless, 87
Light of the Face, 105
Light of the Line, 81,125,
  126
Light of the Spirit, 81,126
Light speed, 59,60
Light's Blessing, 57
Light's Emanation, 104,114
Light's Revealment, 100
Lights of Life and Spirit,
  125
Limitation, 224
Line, the, 20,69,80-82,85,
  88,94,97,108,123-125,
  127,135
Line of Keter, 127

Lines of Limitation, 124
Long Face, the, 105
Love, 220,221
Lower Seven, the, 19-22,41,
  55,56,68,69,81,83,87,
  123,125,127,130,135,
  136,160,166
Lunar Cycles, 20
Luria, Rabbi Isaac, 101,
  126,131,164,180
Lurianic Kabbalah, 146,170

— M —

Macroprosopan, 103
Madame Curie, 63
Maimonides, 226
Majesty, 112
Malkhut, 55,66,79-81,83,
  106,107,112,113,115,
  119,120,123,124,129,
  131,132,133,136,146,
  163,224,225
Masculine, 112
Material Illusion, 119
Material Life, 53
Matter, 41
Meaning of the Bible, 32
Media, 55
Meditation, 53
Meditation (forms of), 56
Mental, Emotional and
  Spiritual, 22
Mesach, 127
Messiah, 27

Messianic Age, 177
Metaphysical, 29,41,61,74,
  84,144
Metaphysical Connections,
  116
Metaphysical Level, 64
Metaphysical Understanding,
  27
Metaphysical Values, 39
Metaphysical world, 86,
  117
Michaelson-Morley's
  experiment, 60,62
Middle Point, 80,86,107,
  108,224
Mind over Matter
  (Power of),39
Mind over Matter, 40,43
Mind, 33,76
Miracles, 38
Mirror of Redemption, 89
Mirrors, 86
Mishmah Torah, 226
Modern Science, 35
Modern Age, 66, 67
Morah Nevukhim, 226
Moses, 164,183,187,188
Mother Earth, 53
Mystical experience, 43

— N —

Native Americans, 162
Nature, 30

Nature of Desire, 91
Nature of Existence, 27,
    61
Nature of Light, 61
Nature of the sickness, 50
Nature of the vessels, 100
Negative, 57, 68
Negative Realm, 56,117
Negative Restriction, 136
Negative Space, 56
Negativity, 23,33,52,55,
    110
Netzah, 103
Neutron, 67
New Age, 26-28,31,33
Newton, 64,143
Nirvana, 102
Non-spiritual, 108
Nuclear disaster, 30

— O —

One World, 155
Optical Illusion, 93
Optical Illusion
    (illustration), 94
Or En Sof, 31,52,54-56,
    70,87,88,103,106,
    115,116,118,119,
    123,124,131,137,
    145,156,157,165,
    166,167,177,180,
    184
Out-of-body experiences,
    41,42

Outer Space, 60,116
Outer Space Connection,
    115, 119

— P —

Pain, 41, 44
Paradox, the, 88,118
Paradox of Resistance, 75
Paradoxical circumstance,
    70
Past, Present and Future,
    21,23, 32, 97
Peace, 25
Perpetual Darkness, 30
Phase of Kingdom, 101
Phases of Awareness, 116
Phases of Creation, 102
Phases of Emanations,
    80-83,96,102
Phases of the Circles, 80,
    81
Physical, 61,74,84,90
Physical Creation, 124,163
Physical Entities, 29
Physical Laws, 85
Physical limitations, 188
Physical Reality, 31
Physical Sciences, 85
Physical Universe, 30,146
Physical World, 29,30,36,
    41,44,54,117
Physicists, 35
Planetary correction, 153

Poison, 46
Politicians, 50,55
Positive Reality, 123
Positive Resistance, 118
Potential Vessel, 112
Power merchants, 33
Prayers, 53
Primordial Man, 127
Process of Correction, 29
Process of knowing, 119
Progress, 53
Prohibition, 47
Propaganda, 50
Psychological, 90
Public Opinion, 29
Purity, 81
Purpose of Creation, 106,
    110,115

— Q —

Quantum Mechanics, 35,37,
    61,63
Quantum theories, 62
Quantum physicist's, 30
Quarks, 67
Quasars, 67

— R —

Radium, 63
Rational Consciousness,
    41,85,118
Rationality, 38

Reality, 31,36,55,97,
    118,119
Realms of Awareness, 124
Realms of Existence, 85
Receiving, 71
Rectification, 31
Reflection, 103
Relativity, theories of,
    62
Religion, 29
Resistance, 74,75,87,142,
    143,144,149
Restriction, 41,52,56,57,
    74,75,76,81,82,110,
    138,176,190,224
Returning Light, 142,146,
    171,201,203
Revealment of Light, 80,
    83,120
Revealer of Light, the,
    82
Revolution of
    Enlightenment, 26
Ritual, 52
Roofs of the Circles, 80,
    86

— S —

Sadness, 108
Sake of Sharing, 55,64,74,
    88,89,119,147,166,
    168,169,171,219,225
Satori, 102

Scientific Era, 67
Scientific Findings, 20
Scientific method, 35,37,
    41,42
Scientist, 59
Sefer Yetsirah, 67
Sefira, 119
Sefira of Circles, the, 81
Sefirot, the, 55, 61,
    113,114
Self-awareness, 99,102
Self-consciousness, 102
Self-deprivation, 100
Sensitive eye, 30
Sensual asceticism, 69
Sharing, 72,74
Six sefirot, 103,105
Slaves, 55
Small face, 103,104,106,
    112
Social Macrocosm, 26
Socio-economic spectrum,
    45
Source, the, 90
Space, the, 41,80,90,91,
    106
Space and Dimension, 85
Space and Time, 84
Space, Time and dimension,
Space, time and motion, 124
Space-Time, 20,21,23
Spaceship, 60
Speed of Light, 20,21,61,
    63

Spiritual, 90,108
Spiritual Adjustment, 31
Spiritual Darkness, 84,88,
    108,168
Spiritual Insurrection, 26
Spiritual Rewards, 74
Spiritual Substance, 26,29,
    79,82,84,85
Star Wars, 67
Stars impel, do not compel,
    40
State of Arousal, 112
State of Mind, 56
State of Consciousness, 31,
    74,124,223
Straight Illumination, 86
Straight Light, the, 80-82,
    146
Straight Line Vessels, 81
Sub-atomic, 61,85
Sub-atomic level, 35,37,38,
    41,42
Sub-atomic particles, 21
Sub-consciousness, 116
Sun, 60
Supreme Presence, the, 87
Suspended animation, 80

— T —

Telekinesis, 39
Television, 55
Ten Sefirot, 163
Ten not Nine, 119

Ten Luminous Emanations, 67,85
Ten sefirot, 120,127,129, 130,135
Ten Circular Sefirot, 224
Terrorism, 30
Thought of Creation, 26, 27,73,147,161,162, 177
Three Columns, 141
Tiferet, 80,103,104,112
Tikune, 68,126,160,163, 165,168,182
Time, 41
Time-Space, 21
Torah, 187
Total Purity, 101
Transcendence, 56
Transference of Energy, 97
Transformation, 101
Traveling in Time, 22
Truth, 117
Tsimtsum, 70,74,75,81, 90,107,114,126,135, 143,145,149,164, 172,224,230

— U —

Umbilical cord, 114
Understanding, 25, 126
Unification, 22,52
United Nations, 154

United States, 50
Universal Gravitation, 64
Universal Rhythm, 20
Universal Truths, 64
Upper Phases, 139
Upper Light, 119,120
Upper Nine Sefirot, 120
Upper Worlds, 80,98

— V —

Vacuum, 90,91
Vessels, 61,102,105
Vessels of Limitation, 156
Vessels of Straightness, 81
Vessels of the Circles, 82
Visible and Invisible Universe, 21
Vision quest, 52
Voluntary, 87
Voluntary restriction, 168

— W —

War on Drugs, 50
Western Culture, 31
Western World, 48
Western Societies, 54,74
Who is wise?, 96

Wisdom of the Stars, 40
Wisdom, 112-115,125,127,
    129
World Peace, 152
World of Action, 82,105,
    164,185
World of Emanation, 105,
    108
World of Formation, 103
World of Fragmentation,
    21
World of Illusion, 20,85,
    108,115,117,156,157,
    190
World of Limitation, 20
World of Resistance, 76,
    23

World of Restriction, 81,
    114,119,147,165,166,
    167,231

— Y —

Yad ha-Hazakah, 226
Yearnings, 90
Yesod, 103
Yohai, Shimon ben, 164,
    219

— Z —

Zaddik, 164-167
Zadikkim, the, 70
Ze'ir Anpin, 105
Zohar, 27,32,40,67,189